DK Guide to
WEATHER

Michael Allaby

A Dorling Kindersley Book

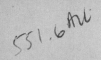

Dorling  Kindersley

LONDON, NEW YORK, SYDNEY, DELHI, PARIS,
MUNICH, and JOHANNESBURG

Project Editor Ben Morgan
Project Art Editor Martin Wilson
Design Team Jacqueline Gooden,
Tory Gordon-Harris, Marcus James
Editorial Team Lee Stacy, Lee Simmons
Managing Editor Mary Ling
Managing Art Editor Rachael Foster
DTP Designer Almudena Díaz
Picture Research Angela Anderson, Andrea Sadler
Jacket Design Piers Tilbury
Production Kate Oliver

First published in Great Britain in 2000
by Dorling Kindersley Limited
9 Henrietta Street, Covent Garden, London WC2E 8PS

2 4 6 8 10 9 7 5 3

A CIP catalogue record for this book
is available from the British Library

ISBN 0-7513-2856-1

Reproduced in Italy by GRB Editrice, Verona

Printed and bound by
Mondadori Printing S.p.A. – Verona – Italy

See our complete
catalogue at
www.dk.com

CONTENTS

RESTLESS PLANET

PEOPLE DEPEND ON THE WEATHER in countless ways. Farmers depend on rain to water their crops, sailors count on strong winds to fill their sails, and holidaymakers take sunshine for granted. Yet Earth's weather is anything but dependable. Our planet's atmosphere is in constant turmoil, a chaotic brew of gas and water kept in motion by the Sun's energy. Sometimes this energy is unleashed with sudden and unexpected savagery – tornadoes can send cars flying through the air, and category-5 hurricanes can turn cities into a wasteland of rubble. Thanks to meteorologists, our ability to predict where chaos might strike next is better than ever, yet weather remains the most deadly natural force at work on our planet.

BLUE PLANET

Water covers three quarters of Earth's surface. Warmed by the Sun, it evaporates and fills the air with invisible vapour. This turns into cloud as it cools, and then falls back to Earth as rain or snow. Without this continual recycling of water through the air, life on land would not be possible. But as well as giving life, water is responsible for the most deadly weather, from hurricanes to killer hail.

FUELLING THE WEATHER

Weather happens because the Sun warms Earth unevenly. Tropical countries receive more heat than the poles, and this imbalance makes the air and clouds in Earth's atmosphere move around constantly. The Sun itself has "weather". Gigantic storms erupt from its surface, hurling scalding gases into space. When these gases collide with Earth they cause the fabulous auroras, or northern and southern lights.

SAVAGE EARTH

The most savage weather happens in storm clouds. A small storm can kill with a well-aimed bolt of lightning; larger storms have more exotic weapons at their disposal. "Supercell" clouds bombard the land with giant hail and spawn tornadoes – ferocious whirlwinds that suck up anything in their path. Over water these turn into towering waterspouts, like this one in Florida. But top prize for savage weather goes to hurricanes, which

MONSOON FLOODS IN CALCUTTA, INDIA

TOO MUCH OF A GOOD THING

Without rain, everyone on Earth would starve. Rain is vital for raising crops, especially the one crop on which half the world's people depend for their staple food – rice. Rice grows in submerged fields, so it can be cultivated only in countries that receive lots of rain. In India and Nepal the monsoon rains make it possible to grow rice in the wet summer, while in equatorial countries rice can be grown all year round. But where heavy rain is a regular occurrence, so are floods. Floods cause more damage, destroy more homes, and kill more people than any other kind of bad weather.

Paddies are fields that farmers deliberately flood to grow rice. Seedlings are sown in mud, then once the crop has ripened, the field is drained and the rice is picked.

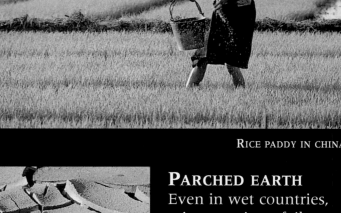

RICE PADDY IN CHINA

PARCHED EARTH

Even in wet countries, rain sometimes fails to fall for long periods. The result is a drought, and this is just as deadly as too much rain. Once-fertile soil turns to dust and blows away in choking duststorms, stripping the land of nutrients. In other places the ground bakes solid and splits as it shrinks. A very severe drought can kill millions if it causes a famine.

Seen from space, Earth is covered by continually swirling cloud.

LIFE IN THE FREEZER

Earth is a planet of extremes. While deserts roast under the tropical Sun, polar regions shiver under a permanent layer of ice. Freezing weather brings its own hazards, such as avalanches, ice storms, and lethal cold snaps. Yet it can also produce weird and wonderful clouds, as well as spectacular "icebows" – rainbows made of ice crystals.

THE ATMOSPHERE

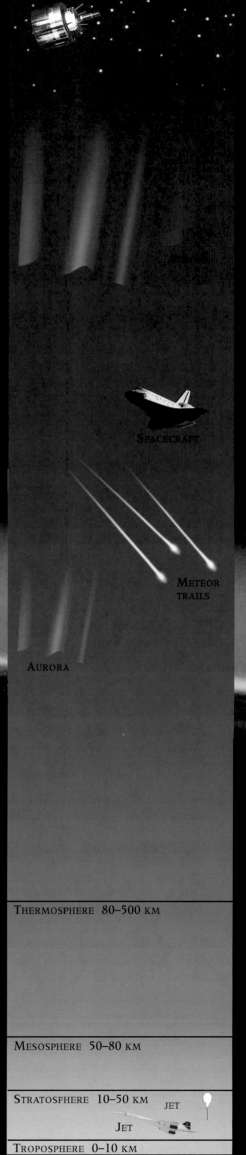

S EEN FROM SPACE, EARTH IS SURROUNDED by a glowing blue haze. This haze is the atmosphere – the blanket of air and moisture, trapped by gravity, that covers our planet and makes life possible. The atmosphere is surprisingly thin. If you could drive straight up in a car, it would take less than 10 minutes to pass through the bottom layer, or troposphere, where all the weather takes place, and only about three hours to reach space. Because of gravity, the troposphere is the most dense part of the atmosphere, and contains 80% of the air and nearly all the moisture. Warmed by the Sun and stirred by Earth's rotation, the troposphere is a continually swirling mass of cloud and air. High above it, the thinning atmosphere gradually peters out as the rarefied air fades into the vacuum of space.

SPACECRAFT

METEOR TRAILS

AURORA

ATMOSPHERE LAYERS

Scientists divide the atmosphere into distinct layers according to temperature. The temperature drops as you go up through the troposphere, but then starts rising as you move through the next layer, the stratosphere. The boundary between these layers is called the tropopause. The air at the tropopause is extremely cold and dry, and there is almost no moisture (and hence no weather) above it.

ABOVE THE CLOUDS

Clouds form in the troposphere. Only the very biggest storm clouds grow tall enough to poke through into the stratosphere. Aeroplanes fly in the upper troposphere or lower stratosphere so they often have to pass through dense banks of cloud during their climb to cruising height. As they break through the layers of cloud they give passengers breathtaking views across the cloud tops.

THERMOSPHERE 80–500 KM

MESOSPHERE 50–80 KM

STRATOSPHERE 10–50 KM   JET

JET

TROPOSPHERE 0–10 KM

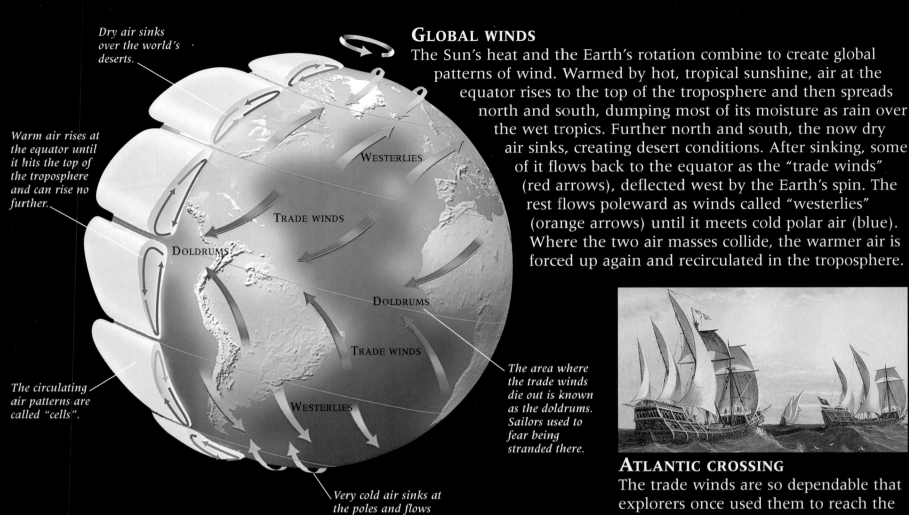

Dry air sinks over the world's deserts.

Warm air rises at the equator until it hits the top of the troposphere and can rise no further.

The circulating air patterns are called "cells".

WESTERLIES

TRADE WINDS

DOLDRUMS

DOLDRUMS

TRADE WINDS

WESTERLIES

The area where the trade winds die out is known as the doldrums. Sailors used to fear being stranded there.

Very cold air sinks at the poles and flows outwards, creating winds called easterlies.

GLOBAL WINDS

The Sun's heat and the Earth's rotation combine to create global patterns of wind. Warmed by hot, tropical sunshine, air at the equator rises to the top of the troposphere and then spreads north and south, dumping most of its moisture as rain over the wet tropics. Further north and south, the now dry air sinks, creating desert conditions. After sinking, some of it flows back to the equator as the "trade winds" (red arrows), deflected west by the Earth's spin. The rest flows poleward as winds called "westerlies" (orange arrows) until it meets cold polar air (blue). Where the two air masses collide, the warmer air is forced up again and recirculated in the troposphere.

ATLANTIC CROSSING

The trade winds are so dependable that explorers once used them to reach the Americas. Italian explorer Christopher Columbus made his first transatlantic voyage in 1492 thanks to the trade winds, and returned by the westerlies.

JET-STREAM

In World War II aircrews flying across the North Pacific found that sometimes they travelled very fast on eastbound routes and much more slowly on westbound routes. Scientists worked out that there must be a very strong wind blowing from west to east right around the world. This is called the jet-stream, and there are two in each hemisphere, both at the top of the troposphere. Even today pilots hitch a ride in the jet-stream, using it to cut hours off the time it takes to fly from the USA to Europe.

JET-STREAM CLOUDS OVER THE RIVER NILE IN EGYPT

THE WEATHER ENGINE

THE AIR AND WATER THAT COVER EARTH work together like a gigantic engine driven by the Sun's heat. The Sun warms Earth unevenly, heating equatorial regions more than the poles. Air and water then spread this heat out, carrying the warmth to the poles via ocean currents and global winds. The constant mixing action, stirred by the planet's rotation, also brings cold air and water back to the equator, where they are reheated. We experience the working of the weather engine as wind, rain, snow, mist, or fog. Underlying all these weather types are a handful of simple, physical principles that govern how air and water mix together and react to heat.

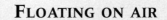

FLOATING ON AIR

When air warms up it expands and becomes lighter, making it rise. This process, called convection, keeps hot-air balloons afloat. A burner keeps the air inside the balloon warmer, and hence lighter, than the air outside, so the balloon rises.

Air is continually circulating between the cold, upper regions and warmer, lower regions of our atmosphere. As warm air rises, it cools. The resulting cold air is heavier than warm air, so it then sinks towards the ground.

When you breathe out on a cold day, water vapour in your breath condenses into liquid droplets. Fog and clouds form in the same way.

INVISIBLE WATER

When water heats up it evaporates – it turns into an invisible gas, or vapour, that mixes with the air. The amount of water vapour that air can hold depends on its temperature. Warm air can hold a lot of water vapour, but cold air holds little. When warm air cools down, its water vapour starts turning back into liquid water, and this process is called condensation. Condensation causes car windows to steam up and breath to become misty on a cold day. The same process also causes fog to form on cold nights, and clouds to form when warm air rises and cools down.

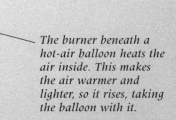

The burner beneath a hot-air balloon heats the air inside. This makes the air warmer and lighter, so it rises, taking the balloon with it.

HIGH PRESSURE

Although air is extremely light, it is not weightless. The weight of all the air in the atmosphere squashing down on us is called air pressure. When the air above us is relatively cold, it slowly sinks and compresses the air below, causing higher pressure. Although high pressure is caused by cold air, it brings fine, sunny weather. This is because the sinking air stops clouds from forming, creating clear blue skies.

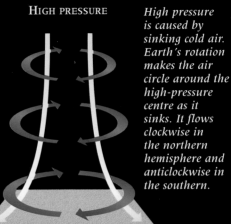

HIGH PRESSURE

High pressure is caused by sinking cold air. Earth's rotation makes the air circle around the high-pressure centre as it sinks. It flows clockwise in the northern hemisphere and anticlockwise in the southern.

LOW PRESSURE

When warm air rises from the ground, it creates an area of low pressure below. Low pressure usually means bad weather. As the rising air cools down its water vapour turns into clouds, which may produce rain, snow, or storms. At the same time, air flows in at ground level to replace the rising warm air, creating windy weather. The weather is much more changeable during periods of low pressure.

LOW PRESSURE

Low pressure is caused by rising warm air. It circulates anticlockwise in the northern hemisphere and clockwise in the southern. At the top, air flows outwards and is carried away.

FRONTAL SYSTEMS

When a mass of cold air from the poles collides with warm air from the tropics, the two do not mix together well and a boundary called a front develops between them. Because the cold air is heavier it slides under the warm air, forcing it upwards and producing clouds. If the air on one side of the front moves faster, a wave may form along the front. This produces an area of low pressure called a depression, and the air moves in a curve around it. Depressions produce swirls of cloud that show clearly on satellite pictures.

DEPRESSING WEATHER
The swirling air in a depression contains a cold front as well as a warm front. The cold front usually moves faster than the warm front and can overtake it, lifting all the warm air from the ground. When this has happened, the fronts are described as occluded.

COLD FRONT

Cold air lies behind a cold front. The front slopes more steeply than a warm front, making the warm air rise rapidly. This often produces towering clouds, showers, and thunderstorms.

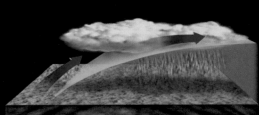

WARM FRONT

Warm air lies behind a warm front. Its slope is very shallow so the warm air rises gently, producing sheets of cloud and rain or drizzle.

CLIMATE AND SEASONS

IF YOU TOOK A JOURNEY from the north pole to the equator, you would discover that there are different patterns of weather around the world. At the north pole the Sun is always low in the sky (except in winter, when it never rises) and the weather is very cold and clear. As you travel south the Sun gets higher and the weather warmer. At the equator the Sun is directly overhead at midday and the weather is hot and humid. The warm air absorbs a lot of moisture from the oceans, which means frequent rain. Weather also depends on the time of year. Towards the poles there are warm and cold seasons, while nearer the equator it is warm all year but there may be wet and dry seasons.

Although the poles have many hours of daylight in summer, the Sun's rays are weak because they fall on land obliquely, like a torch beam held at an angle. As a result, the climate is always cold.

Surface ocean currents are shown here in blue (cold water) and red (warm water). As well as these surface currents, there is a very deep, cold current called the Atlantic conveyor, which takes 1,000 years to circulate from Greenland to Australia and back.

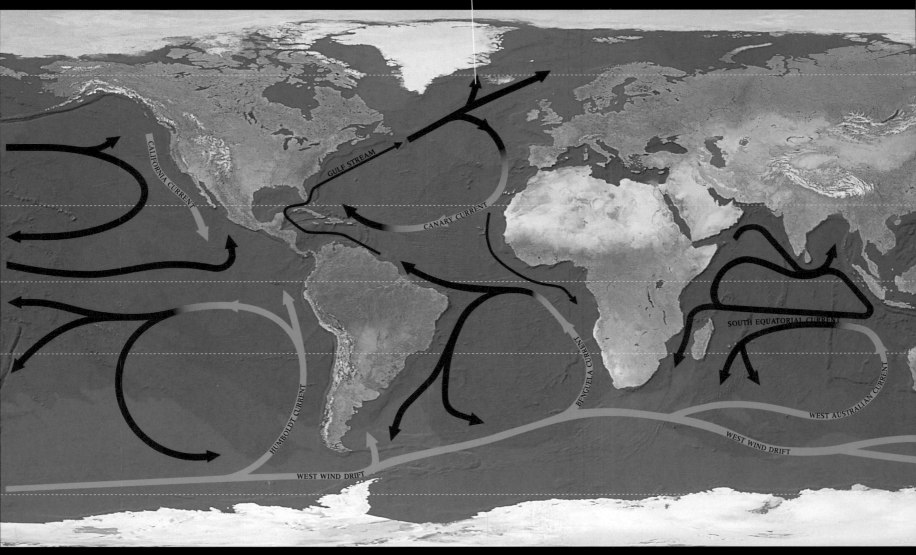

CALIFORNIA CURRENT

GULF STREAM

CANARY CURRENT

HUMBOLDT CURRENT

BENGUELA CURRENT

SOUTH EQUATORIAL CURRENT

WEST AUSTRALIAN CURRENT

WEST WIND DRIFT

WEST WIND DRIFT

WEATHER AND THE SEA

Oceans have an enormous influence on the weather. Water acts as a heat store, absorbing the Sun's warmth near the equator and carrying it towards the poles in ocean currents, which are driven by the wind. For instance, the Gulf Stream, which carries warm water from the Caribbean to western Europe, makes British winters very mild. The warm, moist air associated with the Gulf Stream increases rainfall, so British summers are often overcast. In each ocean the currents form a giant circle, with cold water generally flowing along the western coasts of continents and warm water along the eastern coasts.

CLIMATE

The pattern of weather that a country experiences through the year is known as its climate. The coldest climates are found at the poles, the driest in deserts, and the wettest near the equator, where tropical rainforests flourish in constantly warm and rainy weather. Europe and North America have a temperate climate, with distinct warm and cold seasons. A country's climate depends not just on how far it is from the equator, but also on how close it is to the sea. Central Asia has a very dry climate because it is very far from the sea.

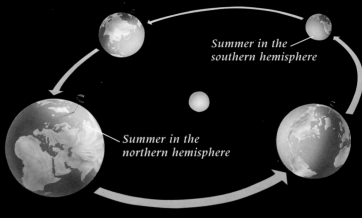

Summer in the southern hemisphere

Summer in the northern hemisphere

SUNNY SIDE UP

Earth spins on a tilted axis as it orbits the Sun. Because of this, first one pole is turned towards the Sun and then the other, and this is what causes seasons. In June the northern hemisphere gets the most sunlight, bringing summer weather to Europe, Asia, and North America. In December it is summer in the southern hemisphere. The equator always receives plenty of sunlight, so it stays hot and sunny all year round.

Temperate climates like that in Europe have mild weather and hot and cold seasons.

Equatorial climates like that in the Amazon rainforest are warm all year round and receive a lot of rain.

Deserts occur wherever rainfall is very low. They may be hot, such as the Sahara, or cold, such as the Gobi.

SPRING

SUMMER

AUTUMN

WINTER

MIST, FOG, AND DEW

EVER WONDERED WHAT it would feel like to walk through a cloud? Without realizing it you have probably already done so, as mist and fog are actually types of cloud that have formed near the ground. On clear evenings when the ground cools rapidly, fog can sometimes blanket the ground in a dense layer up to waist height. Walking through it is a strange experience – your feet disappear in the swirling fog, yet the sky is clear above you. Mist, fog, clouds, and dew are all formed when it is cold enough for water vapour in the air to condense into tiny water droplets.

DEW ON A SPIDER'S WEB

MORNING DEW
In the morning after a cold, cloudless night, the ground – or any outdoor surface – is often covered with millions of gleaming droplets of water, or dew. Dew forms when low-lying water vapour condenses onto cold surfaces. Scientists call the temperature at which water vapour condenses into droplets the "dewpoint".

RESTRICTED VIEWING

The most common type of fog is called radiation fog. On clear nights, when there is no blanket of cloud to trap heat over the land, the ground radiates heat into space and cools down. Because the ground gets very cold, low-lying air also cools. If this air is humid and cools to the dewpoint, its moisture will turn into droplets, producing fog.

MISTY DAWNS

Wooded valleys are often shrouded in veils of mist at dawn, when colder temperatures higher up the valley slopes cause water vapour from the trees to condense and become low cloud. Mist is made from tiny droplets. It is less dense than fog so does not seriously affect visibility. As the Sun warms the ground, the mist gradually evaporates, heralding a clear day.

FOG WRAPPED

Fog soon disperses when the Sun comes up and warms the air. Sometimes the Sun's rays pass right through the fog and warm the ground below. Heat from the ground makes the bottom of the fog evaporate, clearing the air below and leaving a thin layer hovering over the ground. This is called fog stratus.

FOG STRATUS IN THE FRENCH ALPS

IN THE CLOUDS

One of the most famous fog-draped sites is the Golden Gate Bridge, which spans the San Francisco Bay in the USA. For long parts of the day throughout most of August the bridge is blanketed in fog. The fog is caused by the California Current, a current of cold water that runs south through the Pacific from the Arctic Ocean. When cold air rolls in from the California Current it mingles with warm summer air surrounding the bay. The water vapour in the warm air condenses, creating a dense sea fog that is often slow to clear.

13

CLOUDS

HOW COULD YOU DAYDREAM WITHOUT CLOUDS? As you watch their cotton-wool shapes sail across the sky you might wonder what it feels like to fly through one in a hot-air balloon or fall through one with a parachute. In fact, clouds are just like fog – grey and damp inside. Despite the endless variety of shapes, all clouds are made of the same ingredients, water droplets and ice crystals. These are so tiny that they float in the air like dust. Cloud droplets are smaller than specks of flour; it would take four of them to cover the width of a human hair. It is only when the water droplets or ice crystals crash together that they grow large enough to start falling to Earth as rain or snow.

HOW CLOUDS FORM

Clouds form when warm air rises and then cools down until it reaches the dewpoint temperature. This is the temperature at which the invisible water vapour in air starts condensing into liquid droplets. Warm air is forced to rise by one of three processes: by simple convection; by meeting a physical obstacle such as high ground; or by encountering a mass of cold air (a front), which forces the lighter, warmer air upwards.

When air absorbs heat from the ground it expands and gets lighter, which makes it rise (convection). It then cools and its water vapour condenses into droplets.

When moving air encounters hills or mountains it is forced upwards. The rising air cools and clouds form at the dewpoint.

When a mass of cold air and a mass of warm air collide, the warm air is forced to rise above the denser cold air. Clouds form as the warm air cools.

CLOUD TYPES

Although clouds vary enormously from day to day, they can all be identified as one of 10 basic types. Clouds were first classified by the English meteorologist Luke Howard in 1803. His system divided them into clouds that are wispy and hair-like (cirrus), piled and lumpy (cumulus), layered sheets (stratus), or low and grey (nimbus). Each of these types has a number of variations.

Some cumulus clouds mushroom up to 10 km (6 miles) into the sky.

CIRRUS
ABOVE 5,000 m (16,500 ft)

Clouds that are whipped into wisps by steady, high-altitude winds. They are often referred to as "mares' tails".

CIRROCUMULUS
ABOVE 5,000 m (16,500 ft)

Waves or dappled ripples of cloud high in the sky that are made of tiny ice crystals. Sometimes these clouds form a distinctive, scaly pattern called a "mackerel sky".

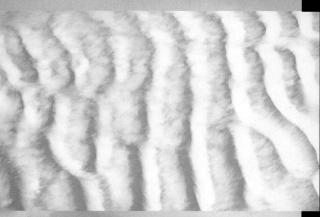

ALTOCUMULUS
2,000–5,000 m (6,500–16,500 ft).

Mid-level, layered or rolling cloud with a ridged structure. Separate stripes of cloud are often clearly visible.

CUMULONIMBUS
600–20,000 m (2,000–65,000 ft)

Heaped cloud with a low base that mushrooms to a massive height, especially in the tropics. Beneath them the sky looks dark. They bring heavy showers and thunderstorms.

CUMULUS
600–1,200 m (2,000–4,000 ft)

Fat, fluffy clouds with a flattish base and tops like cauliflowers. Scattered, fair-weather clouds like these are often seen in summer, but they can pack together to form bigger masses.

STRATOCUMULUS
600–1,800 m (2,000–6,000 ft)

Low-level, grey or white, soft-looking cloud. It forms rounded masses, rolls, or other shapes that may join together in one dense, drizzle-producing layer.

15

WEIRD AND WONDERFUL CLOUDS

Have you ever seen a flying saucer or spotted a strange face in the clouds? Maybe you have been amazed by bright flashes of colour or been spooked by glowing patterns in the night sky? From classical literature to tabloid newspapers, many people have chronicled fabulous sightings in the sky. Often these are clouds that have formed in natural, but unusual, circumstances, such as when air is forced over a high mountain range. Sometimes, however, these curious phenomena are merely the traces created by man-made objects such as aircraft or space rockets.

It's not what you think
Many a reported UFO has turned out to be a lenticular, or lens-shaped, cloud. As air is forced up and down over a mountain range it develops a pattern of waves. Vapour may condense in the peaks of each wave, forming smooth, rounded clouds that remain stationary and "hovering" for hours.

Painted sky
Iridescence occurs when light from the Sun or Moon passes through tiny water droplets or ice crystals in a cloud and is bent into a display of delicate colours. The range of colour depends on the size of the droplets and the angle of the Sun or Moon above the cloud. In this case, the Sun is above the cloud, just outside the photograph.

TRAIL-BLAZERS

Aircraft flying at high altitude can produce clouds called vapour trails. Water vapour emitted from the exhaust of missiles and aircraft as they climb through the atmosphere turns into ice crystals, forming a temporary trail. The lower part of the trail shown above is red because the light has been scattered by dust particles in the air. Winds will gradually disperse the trail.

ANTARCTIC ANTICS

When air crosses a high mountain range, such as the Transantarctic Mountains seen here, it rises and falls, reflecting the shape of the surface. These vertical movements may affect the whole of the lower atmosphere to produce swirling winds. If clouds form as a result, they will be swept and twisted into weird shapes, like this one – a gigantic human ear!

MAKING WAVES

Noctilucent clouds look as if they have waves, like the surface of the sea. They are occasionally seen on summer nights in high latitudes, when the Sun has just dipped below the horizon. The clouds form about 80 km (50 miles) above the ground and are thought to be made from large ice crystals.

WIND AND GALES

Air is forever on the move – sinking, rising, and flowing from areas of high pressure to low pressure. We normally feel these movements as winds or breezes, but sometimes the wind grows fast enough to be classified as a gale. The worst gales happen at sea, but sometimes violent gales unleash their destructive power over land. Between Christmas and New Year in 1999, gales raged across France, uprooting trees and scattering them like matchsticks. Thousands of trees lining the streets of Paris were mowed down and strewn across the roads. Roofs were torn off buildings, traffic lights were twisted out of shape, and broken glass was scattered everywhere. More than 120 people in France and Belgium lost their lives.

WORSE THINGS HAPPEN AT SEA

At sea, where there are no trees or hills to slow the wind, gales can whip up waves big enough to toss boats around like corks and capsize them. In 1805 the British sailor Francis Beaufort devised a scale to measure the wind's force at sea by its effect on waves, and his scale is still used today in shipping forecasts. At force 0, the sea is like a mirror; a force-8 gale produces rolling waves and blows white foam from their crests into streaks; and a force-12 gale – a hurricane – turns the surging sea completely white with foam and spray.

TROPICAL STORMS

In the tropics the Sun's heat fuels turbulent air systems that can produce extremely violent winds. Warm, humid air rising from the sea creates towering storm clouds that are much bigger than those of temperate countries. The resulting storms bring ferocious winds that bend trees and send huge waves crashing on to the shore. Within minutes, a balmy tropical beach can turn into chaos, drenched with torrential rain and battered by raging winds.

LOP-SIDED TREE

In exposed areas where the wind blows mainly from one direction, trees often look as though they have been bent to one side by the wind. This happens because the wind dries the buds, shoots, and leaves on the side facing into the wind. They die, but the other side of the tree is protected and goes on growing.

Driven by stormy winds, giant waves pound La Jument lighthouse in northwest France.

Palm trees are adapted to survive violent winds.

Wind-driven sand will eventually cut through this stalk and topple the rock above.

SAND-BLASTED SCULPTURES

The tremendous force of the wind is nowhere clearer than in deserts, where wind-driven sand eats away at everything – even solid rock, which it carves into fantastic sculptures. Because sand erosion mostly takes place at ground level, towers of rock are carved into teetering pedestals perched on narrow stalks. Where rocks lie in horizontal layers, hard layers will protect the softer layers underneath. This can lead to the formation of a table mountain, or mesa – a spectacular flat-topped mountain eroded only at the sides.

RAIN

WE ARE SURROUNDED BY WATER. Three quarters of our planet is covered by it, and the atmosphere is constantly moving and recycling it. Every day more than 300 billion tonnes of water falls on land as rain. If you tried to drink this much water it would take 10 million years to get through it at a rate of a litre a second. This colossal volume of water does not fall evenly across the continents. Most rain falls in the tropics, where it sustains the world's rich tropical rainforests. On the island of Kauai in Hawaii, for instance, it rains on about 350 days a year. In contrast, the world's deserts are starved of rain. The driest place on Earth is the town of Arica in Chile's Atacama desert, which receives a minuscule 0.1 mm (0.004 in) of rain each year.

In a cloud, water vapour condenses into tiny droplets and ice crystals. These will merge and grow until they are heavy enough to fall.

BURSTING OUT ALL OVER

A big cumulonimbus storm cloud can produce a heavy rainstorm, causing enough rain to swamp a large city in ankle-deep water. As the cloud dies, the rain may become even heavier. The cloud starts to die when its downward air currents overwhelm the upcurrents. Then the cloud releases all its water at once in a cloudburst.

HOW BIG IS A RAINDROP?

Drops come in many different sizes. The smallest is a mist droplet, which is so tiny and light that it just floats in the air. Mist droplets are similar to those that make clouds. Inside a cloud, droplets merge together, like the drops on a wet window, until some are round and heavy enough to fall. A drizzle drop is made from the smallest and lightest drop that will fall. More than 3,000 cloud droplets have to join together to make one drizzle drop. The largest drop, a raindrop, is made of almost 2 million cloud droplets.

RAINING FROGS

"It's raining cats and dogs" is just an expression, but other animals, such as fish and frogs, have been known to fall from the sky during storms. These small creatures can be sucked up from ponds or lakes by tornadoes and carried some distance, before falling to the ground later with the rain.

LIFE FORCE

In many parts of the world almost all the rain falls in one season. Rain pours down on the grassy plains of East Africa in summer, but during the rest of the year dry weather turns plants brown, and the grass disappears. The parched earth cracks, and the trees seem to die. Vast herds of zebra and wildebeest migrate west in search of water. However, when the rains arrive, the grass revives, seeds germinate, and the animals return.

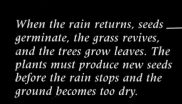

The East African landscape is parched, but the plants are not dead, just dormant and waiting for the summer rain to help them grow again.

When the rain returns, seeds germinate, the grass revives, and the trees grow leaves. The plants must produce new seeds before the rain stops and the ground becomes too dry.

STORM CLOUDS

THE TOWERING CLOUDS that herald a thunderstorm are magnificent to look at, with their thunderous grey bases, topped by billowing columns of cloud. Storms result from the violent mixing of air, water vapour, water droplets, and ice crystals inside cumulonimbus, the biggest clouds on Earth. A single cumulonimbus releases as much energy as the explosion of a nuclear bomb. As well as producing thunder and lightning, storm clouds bring heavy rain or snow, and strong winds that can increase in sudden, unpredictable gusts.

MAMMA FROM HEAVEN

These spectacular clouds are called mammatus ("mamma" is Latin for breast). They form from down-currents of air in the underside of a storm cloud's anvil. When they appear it is wise to find shelter, as they signify that a severe storm with gales and torrential rain is close, and there is a serious risk of tornadoes.

BIRTH OF A STORM CLOUD

Storm clouds develop as warm, moist air rises and cools, causing its water vapour to condense into droplets. Condensation releases heat, which makes the air rise further and the cloud grow taller. A storm cloud may keep growing until it reaches the top of the troposphere. Here, the air temperature levels out and the cloud can rise no further. For about an hour the cloud releases heavy rain, snow, or even hail, until it runs out of moisture and starts to disappear.

Cool air sinks.

Warm, moist air rises.

The anvil shape is normally a useful indicator of the way a storm is heading, as the tail end tends to spread out in the direction of the upper winds.

TROPICAL MENACE

Cumulonimbus clouds are most common in the hot, moist air of the tropics, such as here, above Zaire. Air inside these turbulent giants rises and sinks in currents travelling 50 kmh (30 mph) or more. The strong up-currents can create clouds over 11 km (7 miles) tall – high enough to reach into the stratosphere and show up clearly from space. The top, made from ice crystals, is swept into a huge anvil shape by the wind.

ON THE ALERT
Storm clouds can be visible up to 320 km (200 miles) away, particularly in low-lying terrain, such as here in Arizona, USA. Aircraft pilots steer clear of these clouds as they can be extremely dangerous. If caught in the middle of one, fierce winds can throw an aircraft upwards and then downwards with enough force to make the pilot lose control.

LIGHTNING

YOU KNOW IT IS COMING. The sky darkens. Cats and dogs start acting strangely. Then the storm is directly overhead, a magnificent but terrifying spectacle of blinding light, deafening noise, and pouring rain. A summer thunderstorm releases as much energy as the explosion of 12,000 tonnes of dynamite, and much of this energy is released in the form of lightning. Lightning heats the air to about 30,000 °C (54,000 °F) – five times hotter than the surface of the Sun – and it kills 100 people and starts 10,000 fires every year in the USA. As you read this, about 2,000 thunderstorms are in progress around the world, producing some 100 lightning flashes every second, or more than 8 million a day.

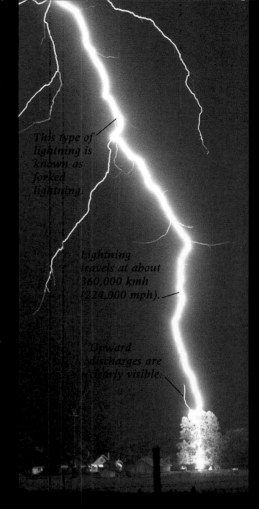

This type of lightning is known as forked lightning.

Lightning travels at about 360,000 kmh (224,000 mph).

Upward discharges are clearly visible.

HOW LIGHTNING FORMS

Inside a cumulonimbus storm cloud, violent air currents cause ice crystals to crash into each other, generating static electricity. The bottom of the storm cloud becomes negatively charged, while the ground and the cloud top are positive. These charges build up until electricity starts leaping between them, at first between different parts of the cloud, and then from the cloud to the ground.

POWER SURGE

This incredible photograph of a lightning bolt striking a tree has captured a very rare sight – two upward lightning discharges, which occur only in the area of a downward stroke. Cloud-to-ground lightning occurs when a downward lightning stroke is met by an upward stroke from the ground. The split-second collision triggers a massive surge of electricity, which heats the air so fast that it explodes, causing the sound of thunder.

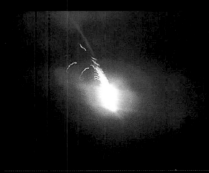

This fulgurite was dug up by someone who saw lightning strike the ground in Avra Valley, Arizona, USA.

TURNED TO STONE

Lightning strikes the ground with so much energy that it heats the soil to about 1,800 °C (3,300 °F) in less than a 100,000th of a second. When lightning tunnels into dry, sandy soil, the heat fuses the soil into the shape of the electricity's path. These curious formations are called fulgurites.

GREAT BALLS OF FIRE

Ball lightning is a mysterious, unexplained phenomenon. It appears from nowhere during thundery weather as a globe of light between the size of a golf ball and a beach ball. Glowing with a dim, yellowish light and lasting just seconds, it floats in the air not far from the ground, and bounces around in random directions.

Light travels faster than sound, so you can tell how far away a storm is by counting the time between seeing the lightning and hearing the thunder. A gap of 3 seconds means the storm is 1 km away (5 seconds means 1 mile).

CLOUD-TO-CLOUD LIGHTNING

As well as flashing from a cloud to the ground, lightning also sparks between regions of positive and negative charge inside clouds, between clouds, and between clouds and the air. This lightning flash between clouds is clearly visible in the night sky above Arizona, USA. Each flash lasts about one fifth of a second and can be up to 5 km (3 miles) long. If the lightning flash is obscured by cloud, it appears to make the cloud glow and is called sheet lightning.

TORNADOES

Fᴿᴏᴍ ᴛʜᴇ ᴡɪᴢᴀʀᴅ ᴏꜰ ᴏᴢ to The Simpsons, tornadoes have played their part in myths and stories. But the terrifying power of a tornado is no legend – this is the most violent concentration of energy that the atmosphere can produce. A tornado can suck up a house and spit it out in splinters, it can lift a whole train from the tracks, and it can tear a child from its parent's arms. Tornadoes are best known for terrorizing the plains of North America, but they are common worldwide, although many go unseen. The UK has about 60 every year.

A funnel descends ominously from the base of a supercell cloud.

At touchdown the funnel becomes a tornado and starts sucking up debris.

A TORNADO IS BORN

Tornadoes form inside huge storm clouds called supercells. These are fuelled by warm air, which is drawn in at the base of the cloud and rises upwards in powerful air currents. Just as water sinking through a plughole starts rotating, so these warm updraughts start spinning round. If the spin becomes sufficiently intense, the rotating air extends below the cloud base as a "funnel". The sight of a funnel sends onlookers rushing for cover – the moment it touches the ground it becomes a fully-fledged tornado.

SPAGHETTI TORNADO

At its base, a tornado may measure just 100 m (330 ft) across, while others spread up to 1.5 km (1 mile) wide. Tornadoes roam erratically but always remain attached to the storm cloud. This one has wandered further than most and is about to lift clear of the ground and disappear.

TORNADO SOUP

The wider a tornado is at its base, the more destructive it is. A giant like this one is capable of generating winds of over 400 kmh (300 mph) because air accelerates as it is drawn into the spinning vortex. The further the air has to travel to the centre, the faster it gets.

LET'S TWIST AGAIN

Tornadoes, aptly known as twisters, are like gigantic, whirling vacuum cleaners that suck up anything they touch, including farm animals, people, and even cars. Doors and windows are sucked from houses, and a really powerful twister will tear a house to shreds and hurl the debris in all directions, creating a cloud of lethal shrapnel. A tornado usually starts life as a white or grey cloud, but the dirt and debris drawn into the vortex soon turn it as black as this one.

WET 'N' WILD

A tornado over water is called a waterspout. Although it looks like a spout of water being sucked upwards, a waterspout is mostly cloud. Even so, it can whip up a huge amount of spray. This one off the coast of Spain killed six people as it dumped tonnes of water onto a pier.

TRACKING TWISTERS

IN APRIL 1974 A CLASS of high school students in Ohio took cover in a ground-floor corridor as a tornado tore through their school with a sickening roar. Seconds later the twister had passed and the noise faded; the students emerged warily to survey the damage. The whole top storey of their school had disappeared, and the school bus lay mangled on the hall stage, as though dropped from the sky. The students had survived a terrifying ordeal – but only just. Such close shaves highlight the need to understand tornadoes and their erratic movements better so that scientists can warn potential victims well before disaster strikes.

○ 3–4 a year
● 2–3 a year
● 1–2 a year
● less than 1 a year   NUMBER OF TORNADOES PER 50-MILE SQUARE

TORNADO ALLEY

Tornadoes are more common in the United States than anywhere else in the world. If you live in the state of Nebraska, Kansas, Oklahoma, Texas or South Dakota, you'll know that you're in Tornado Alley, where tornadoes strike regularly in spring and early summer.

The fruits of the chase – a storm chaser gets a close view of his quarry.

DOPPLER RADAR DISH ON A STORM CHASER'S TRUCK

STORM CHASERS

Some scientists risk incredible danger in order to study tornadoes close up. Their research helps forecasters to give advance warning of tornadoes approaching areas where people live. Chasing tornadoes can also be an addictive and exciting hobby. Enthusiasts not only risk getting caught by a twister, but also risk being pummelled by giant hailstones – all for the thrill of a close sighting.

CLOSE ENCOUNTERS

Tornadoes are difficult to study directly because they destroy weather instruments. However, Doppler radar allows scientists to look inside storm clouds to see the signs of a developing vortex. Incredibly, some people have seen inside a tornado with their own eyes and lived to tell the tale. In 1928 farmer Will Keller was running to his cellar in Kansas when a tornado lifted off the ground and passed over him. He looked up into the funnel and saw lightning dancing constantly within it and tiny tornadoes forming and vanishing in the rim.

IN THE PATH OF DESTRUCTION

When a powerful tornado strikes town it leaves a shocking trail of destruction, but it damages only the ground it touches during its short and unpredictable life. It can demolish a house but leave the house next door standing, though battered by debris. Sometimes large tornadoes give birth to a number of smaller twisters called suction vortexes. A suction vortex can tear one half of a house to pieces and then vanish into thin air, leaving the other half untouched. On open ground these small twisters occasionally lift off patches of dry soil, leaving holes called suction scars that people once believed were giants' footprints. One theory has it that suction vortexes also create the mysterious crop circles often attributed to aliens.

SIGHTS, SOUNDS, AND SMELLS

As a tornado approaches, the wind roars louder and louder until it is as deafening as a jumbo jet taking off. Then comes the crashing sound of debris smashing into buildings with immense force. Scraps of wood and metal are flung through the air like missiles. There can also be freak effects, such as cutlery embedded in tree trunks, or houses lifted from their foundations, turned through 90 degrees, and put back down again. As well as the noise there is a strong stench of sulphur, like rotting food, and sometimes a choking, acrid smell produced by lightning in the funnel.

HURRICANES

DOORS WERE FIRMLY SHUT, windows boarded up, everyone was indoors. A journalist telephoned his report to the mainland: "It's flinging shipping containers about like toys" – then the line went dead. It was 19 November 1999 and Hurricane Lenny was crossing the Caribbean island of St Martin, where it blew away beaches, flooded hotels, ripped off roofs, and washed away roads. Yet even Lenny was rated only category four on the five-point hurricane scale. Fortunately, the worst hurricanes – category fives – are very rare. But all hurricanes are huge and terrifying. They are the biggest, most violent, and most destructive storms our planet is capable of producing.

DOUBLE TROUBLE

This satellite picture shows two hurricanes in September 1999: Hurricane Floyd petering out over New York, and newly formed Hurricane Gert gathering force in the Atlantic. Also known as typhoons or tropical cyclones, hurricanes form over warm, tropical seas in late summer. There are about 40 worldwide each year. Most drift west, bending away from the equator as they move, carried by prevailing winds.

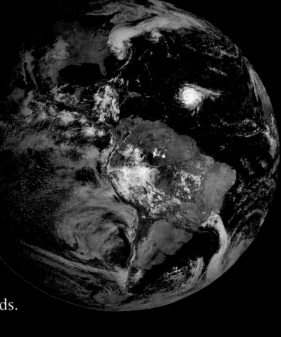

WHAT IS A HURRICANE?

Hurricane Fran, which swerved past Florida in September 1996, was a typical hurricane. Hurricanes form from small storms over tropical oceans. Fed by humid air rising from the warm ocean, and set spinning by the Earth's rotation, they grow into a monstrous, swirling mass of cloud as they drift westwards. The most dangerous part of a hurricane is near the centre, where the wind is so ferocious that it can flatten houses. But most of the damage inflicted by hurricanes is due to floods resulting from torrential rain and gigantic waves that breach the coast.

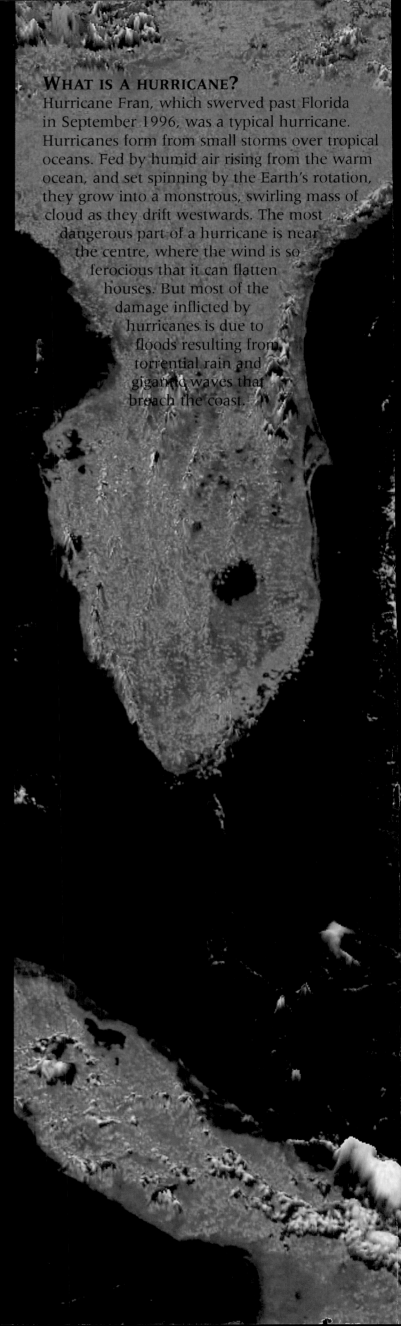

TRACKING FRAN

Thanks to weather satellites, scientists can track hurricanes and try to predict where they might make landfall. Hurricane Fran started life near the coast of Africa and drifted west into the Caribbean, growing in strength as she approached Florida. Then she veered north, eventually making landfall in North Carolina. When hurricanes pass over land they are no longer fed by heat from the ocean, and they soon lose force.

07/9/96
06/9/96
05/9/96
05/9/96

WHERE HURRICANES HAPPEN

04/9/96
03/9/96 02/9/96
01/9/96
31/8/96
30/8/96
29/8/96

WIND SPEED
- 0–63 KMH
- 64–119 KMH
- 120–154 KMH
- 155–179 KMH
- MORE THAN 179 KMH

A hurricane's most deadly winds occur in the eye wall, a circular wall of cloud surrounding a central hole called the eye. Wind speeds can reach more than 240 kmh (150 mph) in the eye wall. But when the eye passes directly overhead, the sky clears and the wind drops to a gentle breeze.

LANDFALL

IT WAS A SATURDAY MORNING when Florida's residents heard a storm was brewing over the Caribbean. At first they were not worried – it was weak and wasn't heading their way. But by evening the storm had changed track and turned into a monster. Hurricane Andrew struck Florida just after 5:00 AM on Sunday, 24 August 1992, becoming the second category-5 hurricane of the century to make landfall in the USA. By the time it left the state four hours later it had caused over $25 billion worth of damage.

STORM SURGE

Most of the people who die in hurricanes are killed by the sea. The low pressure in the eye sucks up the sea beneath, raising it by as much as 6 m (20 ft). At the same time, violent winds whip up waves as tall as houses. The high water level and freak waves combine to produce "storm surge" – towering walls of seawater that surge inland for kilometres, sweeping away boats, trees, and buildings.

The sea level below a hurricane rises due to low pressure inside the eye.

A storm surge causes flooding for kilometres inland.

SHIP OUT OF WATER

Hurricane Andrew tore boats from their moorings, smashed them into each other, and dropped them in piles of mangled wreckage. When the storm surge arrived it carried boats far inland and dumped them. About 15,000 boats were ruined in a matter of minutes.

MASS EVACUATION

TV and radio stations broadcast urgent warnings of Andrew's approach, sending people rushing for safety. More than a million people jumped into cars and fled north. Those who stayed sought safety in public shelters or basements, where they had stored enough food and water to last a fortnight – an essential precaution if they were to find themselves in a devastated wasteland after the storm had passed.

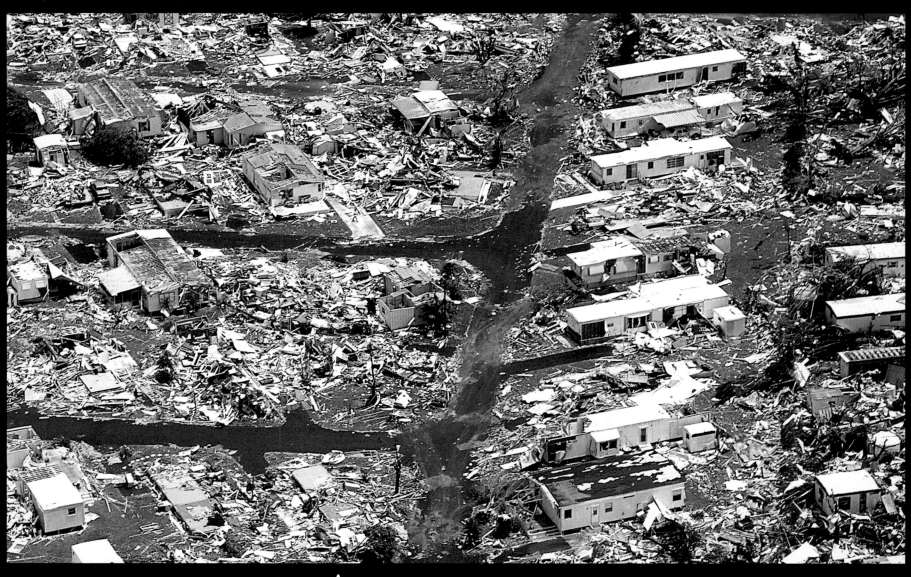

AFTER THE NIGHTMARE

The furious winds in Andrew's eye wall carved out a 40 km (25 mile) wide track of carnage as the hurricane tore its way through the suburbs of Miami. Terrified residents cowered in basements, stairwells, or under tables as screaming winds smashed their windows and blew off their roofs. Mobile homes were mercilessly obliterated, reduced to piles of twisted shrapnel and splinters. Hurricane Andrew completely demolished more than 25,000 homes and damaged more than 100,000, making it the most costly natural disaster in US history. However, thanks to timely warnings and good preparation, only 65 people died. Around 25,000 survivors left Florida for good afterwards.

ACROSS THE OCEAN

Hurricanes soon peter out as they drift away from tropical waters. But in October 1987 the impossible happened – Hurricane Floyd, the last hurricane of the season, crossed the Atlantic Ocean and made landfall in England in the middle of the night. Although barely a category-1 hurricane, Floyd still packed enough punch to mow down 19 million trees and cause £1.5 billion worth of damage. By dawn 19 people had lost their lives.

33

FLOODS

FLOODS KILL FAR MORE PEOPLE and damage more property than any other natural phenomenon. Flash floods are the most terrifying because they are so sudden and violent. A flash flood sends a roaring wall of water surging down a river valley with enough force to sweep away trees and houses and even send giant boulders rolling downhill. But the most destructive floods are those that spread out as far as you can see in every direction, turning dry land into a gigantic lake and leaving thousands of people marooned and helpless.

The Mississippi flood submerged thousands of homes. Many people had to wait on roofs or in treetops until boats came to rescue them.

THE GREAT FLOOD

The Mississippi has burst its banks many times, but the flood of 1993 was perhaps the worst. After months of rain in summer, the Mississippi and Missouri Rivers overwhelmed flood defences and inundated more than 80,000 sq km (31,000 sq miles) of low-lying land. The floods killed 50 people, left 70,000 homeless, and caused damage estimated at $12 billion.

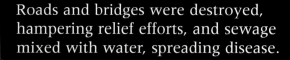

Satellite image of the 1993 Mississippi flood, showing flooded areas in red

HURRICANE FLOODS

Hurricane Mitch struck Honduras in October 1998. A total of 896 mm (35 inches) of rain fell over five days, most of it in the space of just 41 hours. The rain caused floods and mudslides that killed around 11,000 people – the highest death toll from a hurricane in 200 years. Some people were buried alive under the mud, others were washed out to sea and drowned. Roads and bridges were destroyed, hampering relief efforts, and sewage mixed with water, spreading disease.

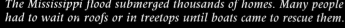

Monsoon rains have turned this stream in Goa, India, into a raging torrent, fed by a gigantic waterfall.

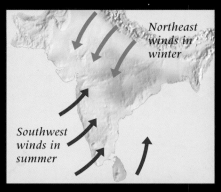

Northeast winds in winter

Southwest winds in summer

THE DELUGE

Summer in India is the monsoon season. Winds from the southwest bring towering clouds that drench the country with rain, sometimes for weeks on end. The rains refresh parched land, but can cause catastrophic floods. In 1997 more than 950 people were killed by monsoon floods in India, and more than 250,000 were driven from their homes in Bangladesh.

MUDDY WATERS

When floodwater rushes down a valley it can carve out so much soil that it becomes a torrent of mud. If the water flows into buildings, the mud settles and can fill a house up to the roof; it then dries and sets like concrete. Although muddy floods cause great damage, they also bring life by spreading nutrients on farmland.

35

THE BIG CHILL

THE ICE STORM THAT STRUCK CANADA in 1998 was one of the worst on record. Five days of freezing rain coated power lines with so much ice that 600 pylons collapsed, leaving 3 million people without power. More than 10,000 troops had to be mobilized to relieve the chaos. Freezing rain is not the only hazard of extreme cold weather. Sudden cold snaps in North America can send temperatures plummeting as low as −50 °C (−58 °F). Wind makes cold snaps even more dangerous, causing a "wind chill" that can freeze exposed flesh in minutes.

RIME FROST
Rime frost forms when small, extremely cold water droplets in fog or cloud collide with solid objects, freezing instantly. It accumulates on the windward side of objects, forming a solid, white crust. Rime is heavy and can cause serious damage if allowed to build up, as on this weather station on Mount Washington, USA.

FREEZING RAIN
A downpour of freezing rain can coat everything with a layer of clear ice, or glaze. Freezing rain consists of large, supercooled raindrops – water droplets that are colder than 0 °C (32 °F) but still liquid. On impact with freezing surfaces they spread out and turn to ice. The weight of this ice can break branches and bring down power lines.

ALL THAT GLITTERS

After a clear winter night, a sunny morning often reveals a glittering landscape covered with crunchy white frost. Known as hoar frost, this consists of a mass of tiny ice crystals arranged in intricate and beautiful patterns.

Hoar frost forms when water vapour in the air freezes directly into ice on cold surfaces without first condensing into water.

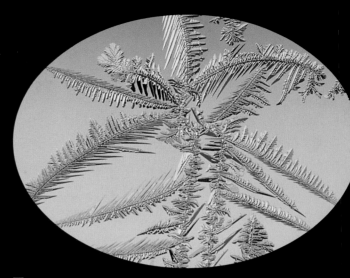

FROSTED WINDOWS

The feather-like patterns that appear on the inside of windows in winter are called fern frost. Water vapour condenses into small droplets on the glass. As these cool below freezing point, ice crystals begin to form, starting a chain reaction in which water freezes onto the crystals' sharpest points, making the crystals grow. Large droplets freeze into patches of ice with no pattern.

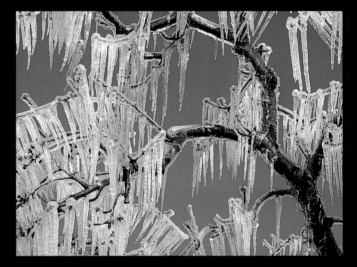

ICE DAGGERS

Winter sunshine is often warm enough to melt the surface of snow or ice, though temperatures in the shade may remain subzero. Melt-water running into a shaded area will refreeze and, as it drips over the edge of a surface, will form a frozen row of drops; an icicle. An icicle grows as more water runs down it and turns to ice.

FROZEN FALLS

In cold winters even waterfalls appear to freeze over. At Niagara Falls in North America, ice grows out from the side of the Falls as splashed drops freeze onto each other. At the same time, huge slabs of ice carried over the Falls build up in the basin, eventually forming a bridge of ice across the river. Until the early 20th century people were allowed on the Niagara ice bridge to witness this spectacle, but in 1912 the ice broke up and swept three people to their deaths; since then it has been out of bounds.

SNOW

SNOW CAN TRANSFORM THE WORLD into a winter wonderland, but it can also be deadly. In the afternoon of 23 February 1999, a slab of snow some 170,000 tonnes in weight broke away from a mountain slope in Austria and started careering towards the village of Galtür. Within less than a minute a gigantic avalanche slammed into Galtür and demolished everything in its path. More than 30 people died, crushed under a torrent of snow and rubble 10 m (33 ft) deep. Snow can also create "white-outs", blinding clouds of snow that reduce visibility to centimetres, causing drivers to veer off roads and walkers to get hopelessly lost in subzero conditions.

Snowflakes come in an amazing variety of shapes, but they usually have six sides. No one has ever found two the same.

SNOWFLAKES

Snow forms when tiny ice crystals in clouds stick together and form snowflakes. When these grow large enough, they fall out of the bottom of the cloud as snow and land on the ground in a jumble, trapping air between them. In fact, snow is mostly air. The largest snowflakes ever seen were at Montana, USA, in January 1887. They measured 38 cm (15 in) wide and 20 cm (8 in) thick. Outside the tropics, most rain starts as snow, but it usually melts before it reaches the ground.

AVALANCHES

Avalanches happen when heavy snow builds up in unstable layers on a mountain. The slightest vibration can set one off – even someone shouting. First the snow slides downhill, but soon it starts tumbling, growing into a terrifying, roaring wall of snow that moves faster than a speeding car. Big avalanches gather up huge clods of earth and boulders, and create a hurricane-force wind ahead of the snow. The wind alone can uproot trees and tear roofs off houses. Avalanches are extremely dangerous – anyone caught in the path of one has just a 5% chance of survival.

BLIZZARDS

A blizzard is a fierce wind that drives falling snow or whips it up from the ground. Severe blizzards hit North America every winter. One of the worst ever was in 1888, when snow piled up to 9 m (30 ft) deep in New York City and 400 people died. In January 1996 heavy snow produced drifts 6 m (20 ft) deep in the city, and people had to cross Times Square on skis to get to work.

BLIZZARD IN TIMES SQUARE, NEW YORK

POWDER CRAZY

For winter sports enthusiasts, nothing beats the exhilaration of speeding downhill through fresh powder, the "driest" form of snow. Skiers even fly by helicopter to find powder and say skiing on it is like floating on a cushion of air. Snowboarders carve up powder into huge clouds, leaving a wavy track behind them. The snow is so soft that falling into it is like falling on a mattress.

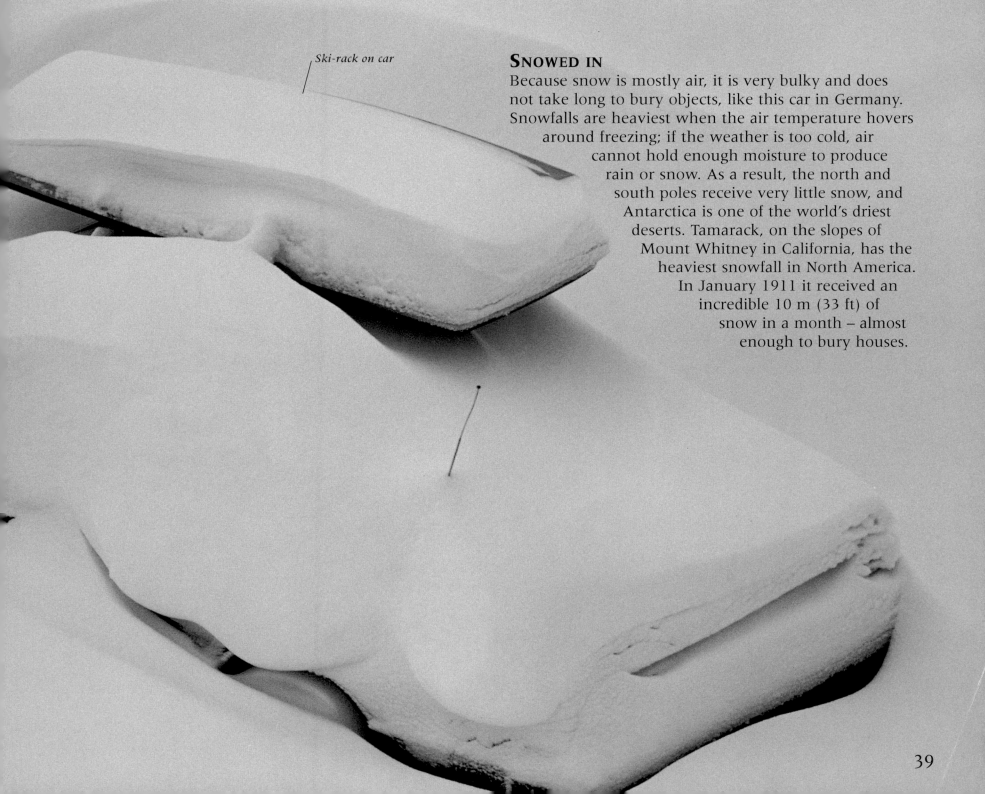

Ski-rack on car

SNOWED IN

Because snow is mostly air, it is very bulky and does not take long to bury objects, like this car in Germany. Snowfalls are heaviest when the air temperature hovers around freezing; if the weather is too cold, air cannot hold enough moisture to produce rain or snow. As a result, the north and south poles receive very little snow, and Antarctica is one of the world's driest deserts. Tamarack, on the slopes of Mount Whitney in California, has the heaviest snowfall in North America. In January 1911 it received an incredible 10 m (33 ft) of snow in a month – almost enough to bury houses.

HAIL

IMAGINE STANDING IN THE MIDDLE of a Nebraskan cornfield at the end of a hot, still summer's day. You look up and notice a great, amorphous cloud obscuring the Sun and casting a shadow across the field. All of a sudden, something thuds painfully on your head. Soon, lumps of ice are falling all around you, pelting the crops with terrible force and falling so thickly that you can hardly see ahead. Hurtling at 160 kmh (100 mph), the hailstones are as big as golf balls – big enough to flatten the corn, to bruise, even to kill. This is exactly what happened in Coffeyville, Kansas, USA, on 3 September 1970, when a violent hail-storm caused immense destruction to crops and property.

OUT ON THE PLAINS

Hail forms inside big storm clouds (cumulonimbus), where the temperature is often below freezing and air currents are very strong. Hail-storms occur everywhere, but they are most frequent and violent across the plains of central USA. This photograph, taken in the desert of Nevada, shows a cumulonimbus cloud with a hail-storm clearly visible below it.

This windscreen has been smashed by a huge hailstone.

HAIL HAVOC

Giant hail causes havoc on the roads, smashing windscreens, denting car roofs, and badly injuring anyone caught in the open. This picture of a violent hail-storm near Shamrock, Texas, USA, was taken from the car of a tornado-chaser, risking massive damage to his car. The cumulonimbus clouds that produce the biggest hail-storms can also trigger tornadoes.

Violent updraughts keep hail airborne.

Warm air is drawn into the cloud.

HOW HAIL FORMS

Hailstones form when ice crystals are blown around in the violent and freezing updraughts (air currents) of a storm cloud. When the updraughts weaken, or the hail becomes too heavy to be supported by the updraught, the hailstones fall to the ground.

Layers of ice

CROSS-SECTION OF A GIANT HAILSTONE

Large hailstones tend to have irregular shapes.

ACTUAL SIZE

LAYER AFTER LAYER

As a small hailstone circulates in a cloud, it is coated with frost as it is carried up to the top of the cloud and then layered with clear ice as it drops into warmer air. This happens repeatedly, coating the hailstone with layers and increasing its size. The more turbulent the cloud, the larger the hailstone becomes.

RECORD BREAKER

Very occasionally, hailstones grow to gigantic proportions, like this one, the largest authenticated hailstone in the world. Weighing 0.77 kg (1 lb 11 oz), it fell on Coffeyville on 3 September 1970. An even bigger hailstone, weighing 1.02 kg (2 lb 4 oz) is said to have fallen in Bangladesh on 14 April 1986 during a hail-storm that killed 92 people. But the worst reported hail-storm occurred in India on 30 April 1888. Hailstones the size of grapefruits killed 246 people, some of whom were completely buried by the hail.

HOT AND DRY

IT SEEMS CRIMINAL TO STAY INDOORS when the Sun is shining and the sky is blue. We usually think of hot weather as something to enjoy, but if scorching temperatures strike unexpectedly, or last for longer than usual, the effects can be disastrous. A heat wave can destroy crops, empty reservoirs, buckle roads, and create the perfect conditions for raging wildfires. And hot weather can kill. The human body copes with heat by producing sweat, which cools down the skin as it evaporates. But if the weather is too hot or the air too humid for sweat to evaporate, this cooling mechanism is taxed beyond its limits. The result is heatstroke, which can lead swiftly to dizziness, collapse, coma, and death.

DEADLY SUMMER

A heat wave sends many people crowding on beaches to soak up the Sun, but others stay in the shade or switch on the air conditioning – a luxury that can save lives. The death-rate in cities rises sharply when daytime temperatures exceed 35 °C (95 °F), especially if it stays very warm at night. First to succumb are usually the very young and the very old, but heatstroke can affect anyone. In July 1996 unusually fierce heat waves in the USA claimed 1,000 lives.

MIRAGE MAKER

Extreme heat can produce tricks of the light known as mirages. This truck looks as though it is driving through shallow water, but it is just an illusion. Air close to the ground is much hotter than the air a little higher, and light is bent as it passes across the boundary between the two temperatures. This creates a shimmering reflection that looks like water.

DUNE-BUSTING

Prolonged hot and dry weather can make deserts spread into bordering areas, burying farms and towns under giant sand dunes as they advance. Schemes like this one in Niger, where millet has been planted in a sand dune, can help to stop the desert in its tracks. The roots of the plants help to bind the sand together to give it some stability, and the leaves act as windbreaks, preventing the surface sand and soil from blowing away.

CATFISH IN A DRYING RIVER, TANZANIA

BURIED ALIVE

In many tropical countries there is a dry season every year, and nature must adapt to cope with the harsh changes this brings. River dwellers, especially, have ingenious means of survival. Some catfish can gulp air, allowing them to struggle through shallow mud to reach permanent waterways. Lungfish and other catfish have an even more dramatic survival strategy. As their rivers dry up they bury themselves in mud, leaving a tiny airhole through which they can breathe. The mud then bakes hard and their hearts slow down. They remain trapped underground until the rains return and free them again.

These two elands died during a drought in Africa, probably as a result of starvation.

DROUGHT

When hot weather outstays its welcome, depriving the land of life-giving rain, it causes drought. A drought can last for months or even years, with catastrophic results. First plants die and crops fail, then animals begin to starve. When food runs out, people begin to starve too. Africa's Sahel region (the area south of the Sahara) suffered a drought that lasted from the 1960s right up until 1980. More than 100,000 people died in the resulting famine, along with 4 million cattle.

WILDFIRES

FIRST THERE IS A SMELL OF SMOKE AND A DISTANT ROAR. Then flames burst suddenly from the top of a tree, and then from another and another. Once the treetops start burning, a forest fire advances literally by leaps and bounds, creating a white-hot inferno of intense heat and clouds of dense, smothering smoke. Burning embers are carried high above the forest and fall randomly, igniting trees ahead of the main blaze. Air rushes in to replace the hot air carried upwards, causing gales and fire-storms that suck even more fuel into the flames. Extinguishing a fire that has taken hold in this way is almost impossible. Wildfires occur naturally – all it takes is hot, dry weather, parched vegetation, and a lightning strike. Occasionally, however, they are started by people, either accidentally or on purpose. Grassland and scrub are often fired deliberately to encourage new plant growth in the ashes.

RAGING FURNACE
Australia suffers from about 15,000 bushfires each year. The bush landscape of trees, shrubs, and grass becomes tinder-dry in the hot, arid Australian climate and is readily ignited by the smallest spark. The worst fires for years broke out in many places simultaneously on 16 February 1983. Driven by strong winds, this "Ash Wednesday" fire spread at terrifying speed, racing through forests and grasslands as fast as a person can run. It was so hot in places that trees literally burst into flames ahead of the advancing fire. The fires claimed 72 lives and left 8,500 people homeless.

OUT OF THE ASHES
Ashes are rich in nutrients, and plants, such as these saw banksia in the Australian bush, soon start to emerge after a fire dies. Some plants actually depend on fire to remove their competitors. Bottle-brush trees in Australia and the jack pine and lodgepole pine in North America do not release their seeds unless there has been a fire, so that the seeds can germinate in the ashes. Other trees burn readily, but then sprout up again from their roots or seeds. Redwood trees survive by having thick, spongy bark that will not burn.

MASS DESTRUCTION

The history of the devastating fires in Indonesia in 1997 began with El Niño, a periodic natural phenomenon causing changes in weather and wind patterns across the Pacific Ocean. A severe drought gripped Indonesia, and when farmers and plantation owners carried out seasonal burning of the dry vegetation, the fires grew out of control. They continued to rage into 1998, casting a pall of smoke right across Southeast Asia. Schools and offices had to close, and on 26 September 1997 an airliner flew into the smoke and crashed, killing all 234 people on board. Eventually the burning rampage was halted when seasonal rains quenched the fires.

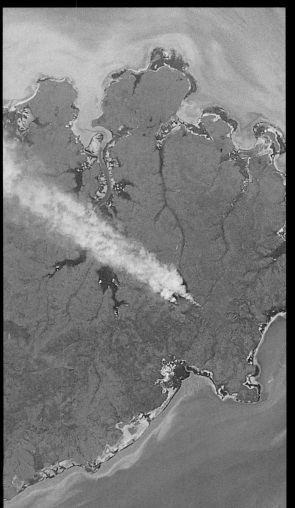

CALIFORNIA BURNING

Wildfires pose a terrifying threat to urban areas. In late 1993 wildfires scorched large areas of southern California, killing three people and forcing 25,000 from their homes. Flames, driven by winds gusting up to 113 kmh (70 mph), burnt timber and brush that had accumulated over six years of drought. Many homes were destroyed before the fire was brought under control on the outskirts of Los Angeles.

DUSTSTORMS

THE FIRST SIGN THAT A DUSTSTORM is on the way is the hot, dry
wind that tears through the streets, flicking grit into the air
and stinging your eyes. Next comes the towering wall of dust –
so tall that it reaches the sky and merges into the clouds. When
the wall of dust engulfs the town, it blots out the Sun and casts
an eerie yellow light across everything. People cover their faces
with scarves and rush indoors, but there is no escape. Shutting
windows and doors may help, but the fine dust gets everywhere.
It gets into food and drink, into people's eyes, ears, and mouths.
It even works its way between the pages of books. Outside, the
suffocating cloud of dust reduces visibility to metres, making
it almost impossible to find your way around.

DUST BOWL

In the 1930s the North American Midwest suffered a
devastating drought that turned millions of acres of farmland
into a parched desert called the Dust Bowl. Once-fertile soil
turned to dust and was blown off the ground by strong winds,
forming choking clouds that killed ducks and geese in midair.
The dust settled on ships 480 km (300 miles) out to sea and it
covered the President's desk in the White House as fast as it was
cleared. One cloud of dust was 5 km (3 miles) high and covered
an area from Canada to Texas and from Montana to Ohio.

THE VIEW FROM SPACE

This picture, taken from a space shuttle, shows a monster
duststorm sweeping across the Sahara in Africa. Small white
clouds have formed at the storm's leading edge, where the
warm, dust-laden air is rising and cooling.
Storms like this can lift dust so high
that the winds carry it all the
way from Africa to
America.

DUST-DEVIL

Dust-devils are twisting
columns of sand and
dust up to 2 km
(1.2 miles) tall, with
winds strong enough
to knock down flimsy
buildings. They develop
over areas of ground
that are hotter
than than their
surroundings. Hot air
rises rapidly over the
ground, and the
surrounding air rushes
in at ground level,
spiralling upwards
and lifting dust as it
approaches the centre.

A cold front meets a body of warm air and pushes under it.

The rising warm air carries airborne dust and sand to a great height.

The air is turbulent and windy under the rising warm air. The winds pick up dust and sand, blowing them into clouds.

HOW A DUSTSTORM FORMS

Deserts are often windy, and a light breeze will lift dust and blow it about. Sand grains are heavier than dust and it takes a stronger wind to lift them. Really violent sandstorms and duststorms happen only when cold air pushes beneath warm air. The warm air rises and the surrounding air rushes in to replace it. This produces winds that blow dust and sand off the ground. The rising warm air carries the cloud of debris to a great height.

SAHARA DOCTOR

The harmattan is a hot, dry wind that crosses the Sahara, absorbing heat from the scorching sand. It can split wood, harden leather, and bake farmland solid. Sometimes it lifts dust clouds high in the sky and then drops the dust, letting it settle everywhere. Despite this, people call the harmattan "the doctor", as it brings relief from humid, clammy weather.

LIGHT SHOWS

THE SKY IS LIKE A VAST STAGE that produces spectacular light shows. The spotlight illuminating this stage is the Sun, which bathes our planet with a brilliant white light. This white light is really a mixture of different colours. When sunlight hits the atmosphere, the colours are scattered in different directions by air, dust, water droplets, or ice crystals – sometimes with dazzling effects. Perhaps the most stunning light show is a rainbow, a vast circle of colour produced by sunlight falling on rain. Rainbows are not real objects, just tricks of the light.

The sky below a rainbow is often brighter than above it because the raindrops here reflect more light.

SEEING A RAINBOW

The best time to see a rainbow is in the morning or late afternoon, when the Sun is out, but rain is falling in the distance. If you stand with your back to the Sun and look towards the rain, you have a good chance of seeing a rainbow. The lower the Sun is, the wider the bow. You can create your own rainbow with a garden sprinkler on a sunny day – stand with your back to the Sun and look through the mist. If you are lucky enough to see a rainbow from a plane you won't see a bow but a whole circle of colours.

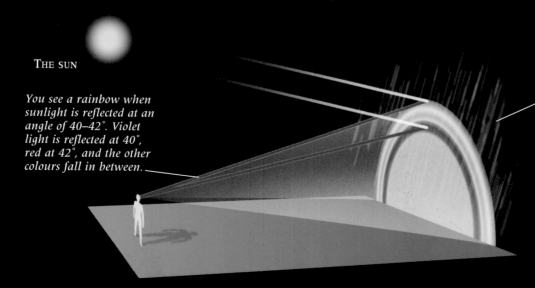

WHY DIFFERENT COLOURS?

We see rainbows because sunlight splits into seven different colours as it passes through raindrops. As light enters a raindrop it bends. The different colours bend by different amounts, which makes them separate. The colours are reflected off the rear surface of the raindrop, then they bend again and separate further when they leave the droplet. Red always appears at the top of a rainbow, followed by orange, yellow, green, blue, indigo, and violet.

THE SUN

You see a rainbow when sunlight is reflected at an angle of 40–42°. Violet light is reflected at 40°, red at 42°, and the other colours fall in between.

The larger the raindrops, the brighter and sharper the colours will appear.

Sometimes a second, fainter bow accompanies a rainbow. It is always a little higher in the sky than the main bow, and the colours appear in reverse order, with red at the bottom. The second bow is caused by light being reflected twice on the rear surface of each water droplet. Some sunlight is lost with each reflection, so the second bow is not as bright as the main one.

ICEBOW

In frozen polar regions, where clouds are made of very tiny ice crystals, you can sometimes see bright white icebows spreading across the horizon. Icebows are produced when sunlight is bent and reflected by the ice crystals. The crystals' small size means that the light rays have no room to spread apart into different colours. Instead, the colours remain close together and the light you see is bright white.

FOGBOW

On a foggy day, if you stand with your back to a low-lying Sun, you can sometimes see a fogbow. Fog consists of tiny water droplets that can bend and reflect light in the same way that raindrops do to produce a rainbow. However, the difference is that a fogbow, like an icebow, appears white. This is because fog droplets are too small to bend light enough for the colours to separate.

SOLAR CORONA

A solar corona is a series of blurry, coloured rings that appear around the Sun. For one to occur, the Sun has to be veiled by a thin layer of cloud. Before the sunlight reaches your eye it passes through droplets in the cloud. In much the same way that raindrops bend sunlight to produce a rainbow, cloud droplets bend and separate sunlight to make a solar corona.

LUNAR CORONA

Sometimes at night the only hint that there are clouds overhead is the appearance of a large bright disc surrounding the Moon. This disc is known as a lunar corona. It occurs when sunlight reflected off the Moon passes through tiny water droplets or ice crystals in thin cloud. The droplets or ice crystals diffuse, or spread out, the white light.

SOLAR WONDERS

RAINBOWS AND ICEBOWS are not the only magical light effects that the Sun and sky can conjure up. Brilliant colours and eerie phenomena – from wavy, green curtains that brighten the whole sky to ghostly apparitions with glowing haloes – can be witnessed if you are in the right place at the right time. This might mean travelling to Alaska, standing atop a very high mountain, or taking a trip in a space shuttle, but if you are lucky enough to see one of these dazzling displays – and don't blink because some of them last only a few seconds – you'll remember it for ever.

CURTAINS OF LIGHT

Auroras (also called the northern and southern lights) are like huge, green curtains, often tinged with pink and blue. They wave gently in the skies above the Arctic and Antarctic regions, and can be as bright as moonlight. They are caused by the "solar wind" – an invisible stream of electrically charged particles hurled into space by storms on the Sun. The solar wind flies through space at up to 3 million kmh (2 million mph). When the particles are about 64,000 km (40,000 miles) from Earth, they are caught in the Earth's magnetic field. The magnetic field carries the particles around the Earth and draws some of them down towards the north and south magnetic poles. High above the poles, the charged particles slam into the atmosphere and collide with air molecules, which absorb the electrical energy and instantly release it as light. The oxygen molecules in air emit a greenish-white light; nitrogen molecules produce pink and blue light.

COSMIC SHOW

The best way to see the aurora is to fly through it in a space shuttle. Seen from space, the aurora forms spectacular dancing curtains of light high above the sky. It seems to radiate into space, but actually the opposite is happening. The solar wind collides first with air molecules in the thinnest, highest part of the atmosphere and works its way down.

HERALDING GOOD WEATHER?

At the beginning and end of cloudy days, rays of sunshine can often be seen pouring out from behind clouds. These are known as crepuscular rays (crepuscular means twilight). The glowing rays are caused by sunlight shining through gaps in the clouds and illuminating dust particles and water droplets in the lower atmosphere. People used to think that crepuscular rays meant the Sun was drawing up water in order to bring fine weather. Unfortunately, such light effects are not reliable predictors of weather.

SCARY SPECTRE

If you are in the right place between the Sun and a cloud, you might see your shadow cast on to the cloud. This rare sight, called a brocken spectre, is seen most often from planes and mountain tops. The spectre may appear huge and terrifying because it usually looks much further away than it really is. Sometimes a colourful glowing ring, or glory, surrounds it. If the spectre is the shadow of a person, the glory appears around the head like a halo.

GREEN FLASH

Occasionally, when the Sun is just about to disappear at sunset, it turns bright green. This "green flash" happens because light from the setting Sun is split by the atmosphere into different colours. Just before sunset, red disappears below the horizon and other colours are scattered or absorbed, until only green is visible.

SUN PILLARS

A vertical shaft of light can appear above the Sun (and occasionally below it) when sunlight is reflected from the undersides of tiny ice crystals falling slowly through the air. These "Sun pillars" are best seen just after dawn or before sunset, when they pick up the rich, orange-red hue of the setting or rising Sun.

SUNDOG

Also called a mock Sun, a sundog is a bright spot of light that appears in the sky to one side of the Sun. This strange phenomenon is caused by falling crystals of ice that bend the Sun's light, creating the illusion of a second Sun. Sometimes there are two sundogs, one on either side of the Sun, and these may be joined by a bow of light called a winter rainbow. Sundogs are often coloured, with red on the side nearest the Sun and a white tail on the opposite side. A similar effect can occur at night, producing "mock Moons".

EL NIÑO

JANUARY IS ORDINARILY DRY IN PERU, but 1998 was no
ordinary year. Time and again, violent storms battered the
coast, bringing torrential downpours even to places where it
had hardly rained in years. Floods drove 22,000 people from
their homes and mudslides engulfed whole villages, burying
300 people alive. And it was not just Peru that was suffering
freak weather. Thousands of kilometres north, storms raged
in Florida and California, causing floods, landslides, and
tornadoes; meanwhile, Australia and Papua New Guinea were
in the grip of a drought during what should have been the
rainy season. The cause of all these events was El Niño – an
ocean current that throws global weather systems into chaos.

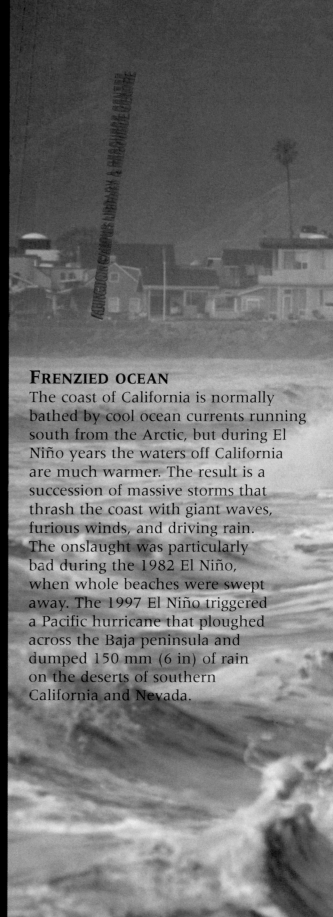

THE BOY-CHILD
Every 5 to 7 years the prevailing
winds temporarily change
direction over the Pacific,
driving warm water east
towards South America.
The warm sea makes the
air more humid, causing
heavy rain and violent
storms. At the same
time, countries in the
west Pacific, deprived of
the warm ocean current,
have very dry weather.
El Niño is Spanish for boy-
child. The name refers to the
baby Jesus because the strange
weather usually begins at Christmas.

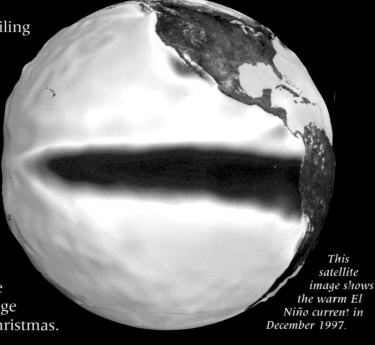

*This
satellite
image shows
the warm El
Niño current in
December 1997.*

FRENZIED OCEAN
The coast of California is normally
bathed by cool ocean currents running
south from the Arctic, but during El
Niño years the waters off California
are much warmer. The result is a
succession of massive storms that
thrash the coast with giant waves,
furious winds, and driving rain.
The onslaught was particularly
bad during the 1982 El Niño,
when whole beaches were swept
away. The 1997 El Niño triggered
a Pacific hurricane that ploughed
across the Baja peninsula and
dumped 150 mm (6 in) of rain
on the deserts of southern
California and Nevada.

FREAK FLOODS
Water rose to roof level in the city of
Eldorado, Brazil, after the rain-swollen
River Ribeira burst its banks in 1997.
Most of the inhabitants were driven
from their homes. The 1997–98 El Niño
also caused floods in the US states of
Washington, Idaho, Nevada, Oregon,
and California, making at least 125,000
people homeless. Of the 30 or so El
Niños that occurred in the 20th century,
this was the most violent. It was also the
most expensive in history, causing an
estimated $20 billion worth of damage.

MUDSLIDE!

When prolonged heavy rain soaks into
the ground, the earth turns into a soupy
sludge. On steep, treeless slopes this
waterlogged mass of mud may succumb
to gravity and start slipping downhill,
carrying everything with it – including
roads and houses. Mudslides can shift
thousands of tonnes of earth in seconds
and carry enough force to smash through
anything in their path. The mudslides
caused by the 1997–98 El Niño in South
America were all the worse because of
widespread deforestation in the region

VOLCANIC WEATHER

IN 1815, WITH A ROAR THAT COULD BE HEARD hundreds of kilometres away, Mount Tambora in Indonesia exploded. The eruption – the most violent on record – obliterated the top third of the mountain and blasted some 145 cubic kilometres (35 cubic miles) of rock, dust, and ash into the sky, producing a cloud of debris so gigantic that it injected material into the stratosphere. Volcanic eruptions such as Tambora can have profound effects on weather across the planet. As well as triggering catastrophic tidal waves and landslides, they can launch so much dust into the upper atmosphere that skies darken around the world, robbing the ground of life-giving sunlight. People called 1816 "the year with no summer". While parts of the USA and Canada had frost and snow through summer, cold and miserable weather in western Europe caused crop failures and famine.

The eruption of Mount St Helens blew the top 400 m (1,300 ft) off the mountain and lifted half a cubic km (0.1 cubic mile) of debris into the atmosphere.

MOUNT ST HELENS

In the spring of 1980 the northern flank of Mount St Helens in the USA began to bulge ominously as pressure welled deep inside the volcano. On 18 May the inevitable happened. The northern slope collapsed, releasing a jet of superheated gas that blasted rock and ash sideways out of the mountain, flattening 10 million trees and producing a colossal cloud of debris. Next came the vertical eruption, which smashed the summit and threw ash and gas 19 km (12 miles) high. Carried by high winds, the ash from Mount St Helens encircled the entire planet, producing hazy skies, stunning red sunsets, and a brief drop in temperature worldwide.

MOUNT PINATUBO

When Mount Pinatubo exploded in the Philippines in 1991, a torrent of scalding ash incinerated the surrounding land for kilometres. Clouds of debris 40 km (25 miles) high blackened the sky and covered huge areas with ash, turning everything grey. Rain turned the ash into mud, causing mudslides that destroyed thousands of people's homes. Pinatubo's eruption was the most violent of the 20th century and killed nearly 800 people.

The Philippines

SATELLITE PICTURE
OF VOLCANIC CLOUD
FROM PINATUBO

GLOBAL COOLING

As well as belching out clouds of ash and molten rock, Pinatubo belched out a mass of volcanic dust and gas into the stratosphere. More than 15 million tonnes of sulphur dioxide formed clouds of tiny sulphuric acid droplets, which spread around the world and lingered in the air for over 18 months. The droplets blocked out sunlight, making temperatures around the world about 0.5 °C (0.9 °F) lower than usual.

VOLCANIC SUNSETS

Volcanoes can produce amazing sunsets. Tiny particles of volcanic ash scatter all of the colours in sunlight except red and orange, which pass through. The effect is greatest when the Sun is low in the sky and light has to pass through a lot of dusty air. Volcanic sunsets continue until all the dust has settled. They were seen around the world for months after Mount St Helens's eruption.

WEATHER FORECASTING

THE TV FORECASTER WHO TELLS US what the weather will be like is backed by teams of meteorologists (weather scientists), instruments located all over the world and above it, and some of the biggest and most powerful computers in existence. The first weather forecasts were issued in 1869 in the USA. They were compiled from observations sent by telegraph to a central office and calculations made with pen and paper. Today there is a global network of observing stations on land and at sea, satellites maintaining a constant watch over every part of the Earth, and radio and e-mail for the instant transmission of information.

WEATHER STATIONS

There are some 10,000 surface weather stations around the world like this one in Idaho, USA. Most are on land, but some are on moored ships in the middle of the sea. Weather stations send reports to a forecasting centre four times a day, giving details of cloud type, wind speed, temperature, pressure, and so on.

The GOES satellites orbit at a height of 36,000 km (23,000 miles).

THERE SHE GOES

Weather satellites orbit Earth taking pictures, monitoring the temperature, and even measuring the height of waves. The USA's weather satellites are called GOES (geostationary operational environmental satellites). They orbit at the same speed as Earth rotates, so they always stay over the same point. Other satellites are in polar orbits, which take them over the north and south poles alternately.

WEATHER BALLOON

At many weather stations, weather balloons are released each day at noon and midnight Greenwich Mean Time. They rise about 20–30 km (12–19 miles), then burst. The balloon's drift shows wind speed and direction. Beneath it, on a long cable, is a package of instruments that measure temperature, pressure, and humidity, and radio their readings to the ground station. When the balloon bursts, the instruments descend on a parachute.

NUMBER-CRUNCHING

The data from weather stations and satellites is fed into powerful supercomputers. These perform millions of calculations as they predict how the weather will change. Supercomputers are a massive improvement over pen and paper, but the weather is so complicated that it cannot be accurately predicted for more than a few days ahead.

ABINGDON CAMPUS LIBRARY & RESOURCE CENTRE

SPIES IN THE SKY

This is North America as it appeared to one of the GOES satellites on 10 February 2000. The swirling cloud masses are areas where it may be stormy or rainy; where the land or coastline is clear, such as over Florida, the weather is fine. GOES satellites transmit their data to ground stations every 30 minutes. The pictures are uploaded onto the Internet, allowing anyone in the world to get an updated view of the continent's weather.

WEATHER MAPS

Forecasts are shown on special maps. Black lines on a weather map join places with the same air pressure; black circles show where pressure is high or low. Blue triangles are cold fronts, red semicircles are warm fronts, and a mixture of triangles and semicircles is an occluded front.

The Quickscat satellite measures wind speeds.

RESEARCH

Scientists also use weather satellites to study how Earth's climate and weather work. This satellite image shows wind patterns over the Pacific Ocean. By studying such patterns, meteorologists hope to improve forecasts of hurricane and iceberg movements, and so give ships and coastal inhabitants better warning of approaching danger.

POLLUTION

FOR FOUR DAYS IN DECEMBER 1952 a lethal concoction of fog mixed with smoke and soot from thousands of coal fires and steam trains engulfed London. Visibility was reduced to a few metres, streetlights came on in the middle of the day, and buses crawled at barely walking pace. People choked and spluttered as they walked, finding it difficult to breathe, and 4,000 people died, poisoned by the air. This kind of thick, toxic smog was once common in industrial cities. Since then, global concern has led to the introduction of laws to clean up urban air, but vehicle exhaust and industrial waste are still polluting the atmosphere and having a dramatic effect on life on Earth.

ACID RAIN

This conifer forest is suffering from the effects of acid rain. Acid rain occurs when sulphur and nitrogen oxides, released by factories and cars, interact with sunlight and water vapour in the clouds to form sulphuric and nitric acids. The airborne acid contaminates water supplies, takes vital nutrients from soil, and damages forests and crops. It can also kill fish and other freshwater animals in lakes and rivers. The problem is particularly bad in North America and northwest Europe.

OZONE HOLE

About 25–50 km (15–30 miles) up in the Earth's atmosphere is a thin layer of the gas ozone. The ozone layer protects life on Earth from harmful ultraviolet radiation from the Sun. In the 1980s, scientists discovered that a hole develops in the ozone layer over Antarctica each spring. They traced the cause to chemicals released by aerosol can propellants, fridges, and air conditioners. The combination of cold weather and bright sunlight causes these chemicals to destroy ozone

POLLUTION IN MEXICO

Mexico City suffers from extreme photochemical smog. This forms when gases from vehicle exhausts react in strong sunlight, producing substances that reduce visibility and make the air difficult to breathe. Mexico City's smog is particularly bad because the town is surrounded by a ring of mountains that trap the polluted air.

GLOBAL WARMING

By the year 2025 there will be more than a billion cars on the roads, each belching out carbon dioxide and other exhaust fumes. Scientists fear that the rising level of carbon dioxide in the atmosphere is trapping the Sun's heat and causing a gradual warming of the world's climates (global warming). The effect of this may not just be hotter weather, but more extreme weather – increased rain and storms in some areas, and drier weather in others. It might even alter ocean currents. If the Gulf Stream changed course, for instance, northwest Europe would get much colder.

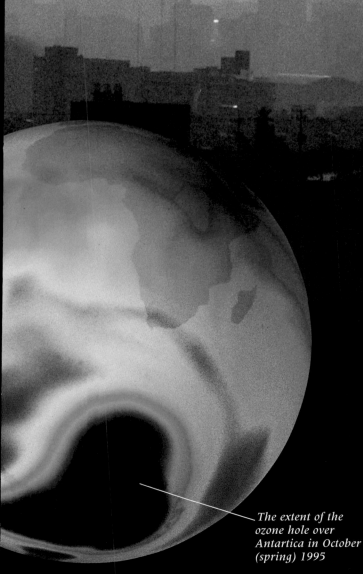

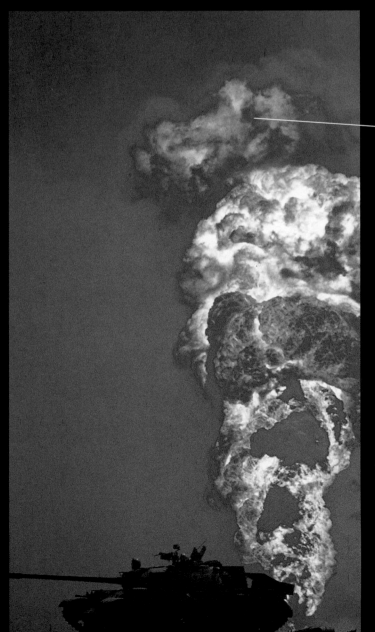

A billowing tower of fire and smoke from a burning oil well in Kuwait

GULF WAR FIRES

In 1990, during the Gulf War between United Nations forces and Iraq, oil refineries and storage depots at the northern end of the Persian Gulf were set on fire. They belched out so much black smoke that it was seen clearly by orbiting satellites and cast a shadow over the Earth's surface. The smoke soon cleared and, alarming though the spectacle was, it had no lasting effect on the weather.

The extent of the ozone hole over Antartica in October (spring) 1995

HARNESSING WEATHER

EVERY DAY THE SUN FLOODS EARTH with 20 times more energy than is used by all the world's people in a year. Much of this energy is absorbed and released by the atmosphere. A rain shower, for instance, releases as much energy as New York City's streetlights use in a night. If scientists could somehow tap into this tremendous source of power, they could solve humanity's energy needs forever. Think of the coal, oil, gas, and nuclear fuel we would save if we could harness weather instead. Unfortunately, achieving this dream has proved far from easy.

SOLAR POWER

The problem with trying to capture the Sun's energy is that it is spread over a vast area. To get round this, solar power stations use thousands of wide mirrors to collect and concentrate as much sunlight as possible. This solar power station in California's Mojave Desert is part of a vast network that uses a total of 650,000 solar mirrors. The desert climate is ideal for solar power, but in other parts of the world cloudy skies make solar power less effective.

WIND FARM

These windmills belong to a wind farm in California that turns the wind's energy into electricity. The windmills must be far apart so that they do not steal wind from each other, and it takes around 3,000 of them to generate as much power as a coal power station. Wind farms only work in exposed places such as hilltops or coasts. Although they do not cause pollution, some people think they spoil the natural look of such wild places.

WIND GAMES

Wind may not drive the wheels of industry, but it provides endless fun. These spectacular kites at a kite fair could not fly without wind to lift them. Windsurfing, sailing, and land-yachting all depend on the wind, and hot-air balloonists and hang-gliders need the wind to carry them. Even surfers and body-boarders need wind because it is the wind that creates waves.

SUNNY DELIGHT

Bowl-shaped solar mirrors are called heliostats. They focus sunlight onto a central target, which gets very hot. Heliostats are expensive to build, work only in places with guaranteed sunshine, and yet they generate very little energy. In sunny countries many people have solar collectors on their roofs to heat water for showers and laundry. These are like trays containing pipes running back and forth. The collectors are black to absorb heat, and the heat warms water in the pipes. The pipes pass through a water tank indoors and warm the water.

Each of these computer-controlled mirrors tracks the Sun across the sky and reflects its heat onto tubes filled with oil. The heated oil is then used to boil water and make steam, and the steam drives a machine called a turbine to generate electricity.

FLOUR POWER

Sunshine and rain are vital for growing the crops that we depend on, such as this wheat, ripening on a North American farm. But crops can also be used to produce alternatives to petrol, and this is perhaps the most efficient way to use solar energy. In some countries, sugar extracted from maize, sugar beet, or potatoes is converted into alcohol by fermentation. The alcohol is then used as a fuel in specially adapted cars. Fast-growing plants like willow can also be used to fuel power stations.

WIND CATEGORIES: THE BEAUFORT SCALE

Force	Wind speed (mph)	Description	Effects
0	0.1 or less	Calm	Air feels still; smoke rises vertically.
1	1–3	Light air	Wind vanes and flags do not move, but rising smoke drifts.
2	4–7	Light breeze	Drifting smoke indicates the wind direction.
3	8–12	Gentle breeze	Leaves rustle, small twigs move, and lightweight flags stir gently.
4	13–18	Moderate breeze	Loose leaves and pieces of paper blow around.
5	19–24	Fresh breeze	Small trees that are in full leaf sway.
6	25–31	Strong breeze	Difficult to use an umbrella.
7	32–38	Moderate gale	The wind exerts strong pressure on people walking into it.
8	39–46	Fresh gale	Small twigs torn from trees.
9	47–54	Strong gale	Chimneys blown down; slates and tiles torn from roofs.
10	55–63	Whole gale	Trees broken or uprooted.
11	64–75	Storm	Trees uprooted and blown some distance, cars overturned.
12	above 75	Hurricane	Devastation widespread, buildings destroyed, and many trees uprooted.

HURRICANE CATEGORIES: THE SAFFIR/SIMPSON SCALE

Category	Wind speed (mph)	Damage
1	74–95	Trees and shrubs lose leaves and twigs; unanchored mobile homes damaged.
2	96–110	Small trees blown down, major damage to exposed mobile homes, chimneys and tiles blown from roofs.
3	111–130	Leaves stripped from trees, big trees blown down, mobile homes destroyed, small buildings damaged structurally.
4	131–155	Extensive damage to windows, roofs, and doors; mobile homes completely demolished; floods up to 10 km (6 miles) inland.
5	Above 155	All buildings severely damaged, small buildings destroyed.

TORNADO CATEGORIES: THE FUJITA SCALE

Number	Wind speed (mph)	Effects
F0	40–72	Light damage. Branches broken from trees.
F1	73–112	Moderate damage. Trees snap, windows break, some roof damage.
F2	113–157	Considerable damage. Large trees uprooted, flimsy buildings destroyed.
F3	158–206	Severe damage. Trees flattened, cars overturned, walls demolished.
F4	207–260	Devastating damage. Frame houses demolished.
F5	261–318	Incredible damage. Cars moved more than 90 m (300 ft), steel-reinforced buildings badly damaged.

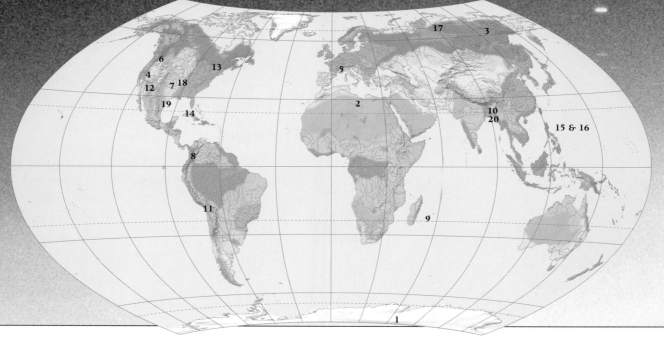

MAP OF WEATHER RECORDS

1. Coldest place
Vostok Station, Antarctica. On 21 July 1983 the temperature was measured as –89.2 °C (–128.6 °F).

2. Hottest place
El Azizia, Libya. On 13 September 1922 the temperature reached 57.8 °C (136 °F).

3. Greatest extremes
Verkhoyansk, Siberia. The lowest recorded temperature is –68 °C (–90 °F), the highest is 37 °C (98 °F).

4. Heaviest snowstorm
Mount Shasta Ski Bowl, California, USA. One storm, lasting from 13 to 19 December 1955, delivered 480 cm (189 in) of snow.

5. Snowiest day
Bessans, France. 173 cm (68 in) of snow fell in 19 hours on 5–6 April 1969.

6. Snowiest place
Mount Baker, Washington State, USA, received 29 m (95 ft) of snow in the winter of 1998–99.

7. Biggest hailstone
The largest authenticated hailstone fell at Coffeyville, Kansas, USA, on 3 September 1970 and measured 14.4 cm (5.7 in) wide and 0.77 kg (1 lb 11 oz) in weight. There are also reports of hailstones 1 kg (2 lb 4 oz) in weight (as heavy as a bag of sugar) falling at Gopalganj in Bangladesh on 14 April 1986.

8. Rainiest place
Lloro, Colombia, is estimated to have received an average 1,330 cm (524 in) of rain a year for 29 years.

9. Rainiest day
On 15–16 March 1952, 187 cm (74 in) of rain fell on the island of Reunion in the Indian Ocean.

10. Wettest year
Between August 1860 and July 1861 Cherrapunji, India, received approximately 26 m (86 ft) of rain.

11. Driest place
Arica in Chile's Atacama Desert had an average of less than 0.75 mm (0.03 in) of rain a year over 59 years.

12. Longest drought
Southwestern North America suffered a 59-year drought from 1246 to 1305. It was most intense between 1276 and 1299.

13. Strongest recorded wind gust
372 kmh (231 mph) at Mount Washington, New Hampshire, USA, on 12 April 1934. The winds in tornadoes can be even faster.

14. Strongest sustained wind
About 322 kmh (200 mph), when the Labor Day Storm struck the Florida Keys, USA, on 2 September 1935.

15. Fiercest hurricane
Typhoon Tip, in the northwest Pacific on 12 October 1979, had sustained winds of 305 kmh (190 mph).

16. Lowest air pressure
Pressure in the eye of Typhoon Tip was 870 millibars.

17. Highest air pressure
A pressure of 1,083.8 millibars was recorded at Agata, Siberia, Russia, on 31 December 1968.

18. Most severe tornado outbreak
In March 1925 a series of possibly seven tornadoes (the Tri-state Tornado) crossed Missouri, Illinois, and Indiana, covering 703 km (437 miles) and killing 689 people.

19. Worst American hurricane
At Galveston, Texas, on 8 September 1900, a hurricane killed 6,000 people, injured more than 5,000, and destroyed half the town's buildings.

20. Worst cyclone
In November 1970 a cyclone moved from the Bay of Bengal across Bangladesh, causing floods that killed about half a million people.

1697 In October a castle exploded in the town of Athlone, Ireland, when lightning set fire to a store room containing 260 barrels of gunpowder.

1876–9 Between 9 and 13 million people starved to death in northern China as a result of one of the worst droughts in history.

1879 The Tay Bridge in Scotland was struck by two tornadoes simultaneously on 28 December. The bridge was destroyed and the evening mail train from Edinburgh to Dundee fell into the river. Between 75 and 90 people were killed.

1887 The Yellow River in China burst its banks and flooded about 26,000 sq km (10,000 sq miles) in September and October. Between 900,000 and 2.5 million people died.

1888 A hailstorm pummelled the town of Moradabad in India with hailstones the size of grapefruits, killing 246 people and over 1,000 sheep and goats.

1925 The "Tri-state Tornado" – the worst tornado disaster in US history – ploughed through the states of Missouri, Illinois, and Indiana, leaving a trail of devastation 1.5 km (0.9 miles) wide and killing 689 people. The Tri-state Tornado was probably a series of up to seven separate tornadoes. The death toll was unusually high because the tornadoes passed through a string of mining villages and farms, moving so swiftly that they caught people unawares.

1930s The North American Midwest had almost no rain for five years, turning thousands of square kilometres of farmland into a desert called the Dust Bowl. Hot winds whipped up the parched soil, causing choking duststorms. Around 5,000 people died as a result of heatstroke and breathing problems.

1931 The Yangtze River, China, rose 30 m (97 ft) following a period of heavy rain. About 3.7 million people died, some in the floods but most in the famine that followed.

1962 In January a huge block of ice broke off a glacier on Mount Huascaran in Peru. It fell a kilometre and then crashed into a snowfield, triggering a massive avalanche and mudslide that destroyed a town and six villages. Approximately 4,000 people were killed.

1963 In December a bolt of lightning struck the wing of a Boeing 707 aircraft over Maryland, USA, and set light to the fuel tank. The plane exploded in midair, killing 81 people.

1970 Half a million people died in Bangladesh in November when a tropical cyclone produced a gigantic wave that flooded the Ganges Delta.

1974 Cyclone Tracy destroyed 90% of the city of Darwin, Australia, on Christmas Day. More than 50 people died.

1976 Hurricane Liza struck La Paz, Mexico, on 1 October. Heavy rain destroyed a dam, releasing a wall of water that killed at least 630 people in a shanty town downstream.

1977 A cyclone and storm surge washed away 21 villages and damaged 44 more in Andhra Pradesh, India, on 19 November. An estimated 20,000 people died and more than 2 million were made homeless.

1977 A cyclone killed at least 1,500 people and destroyed more than 500,000 buildings in Sri Lanka and southern India on 23 November.

1980 A heat wave lasting more than a month hit a vast area of the USA in the summer. In Texas, temperatures exceeded 38 °C (100 °F) almost every day. The scorching weather started forest fires, withered crops, buckled roads, and dried up reservoirs. The official death toll was 1,265.

1982 Monsoon floods in Orissa, India, in September killed at least 1,000 people and left 5 million marooned on roofs and high ground.

1983 Searing summer temperatures triggered hundreds of forest fires in southern Australia in February. The fires raged out of control, sending burning shreds of vegetation into the air that spread the blaze. Fire engulfed the mainly wood-built town of Macedon, killed more than 70 people, and damaged thousands of acres of land.

1984 Giant hailstones pelted the town of Munich, Germany, for just 20 minutes on 12 July, causing an incredible $1 billion worth of damage and injuring more than 400 people. The hail punched holes in roofs, smashed car windows, flattened greenhouses and wrecked more than 150 aircraft at the city's airport.

1985 A cyclone and storm surge struck islands off Bangladesh on 25 May, killing an estimated 2,540 people, but possibly as many as 11,000.

1988 Monsoon floods inundated 75% of Bangladesh in late August and September, killing more than 2,000 people and leaving at least 30 million homeless.

1988 Hurricane Gilbert killed at least 260 people in the Caribbean and the Gulf of Mexico between 12 and 17 September, and generated nearly 40 tornadoes in Texas.

1991 A cyclone killed at least 131,000 people on coastal islands off Bangladesh on 30 April.

1992 Blizzards caused avalanches that killed 201 people in Turkey in February.

1992 Hurricane Andrew struck the Bahamas, Florida, and Louisiana in August, killing 65 people, destroying 25,000 homes, and almost completely demolishing the towns of Homestead and Florida City, Florida. It was the most costly hurricane in US history, with damage estimated at $20 billion.

1993 A blizzard from 12 to 15 March killed at least 238 people in the eastern United States, 4 in Canada, and 3 in Cuba.

1993 Mudslides killed 400 people and destroyed 1,000 homes in Honduras from 31 October to 2 November.

1995 A mudslide destroyed a village in Afghanistan on 27 March, killing 354 people.

1996 A tornado in Bangladesh destroyed 80 villages in less than half an hour on 13 May, killing more than 440 people and injuring more than 32,000.

1997 An avalanche buried at least 100 people in northern Afghanistan on 26 March. The victims had been walking along a road to catch a bus.

1997 Lightning killed 19 people and injured 6 in Andhra Pradesh, India, on 11 September.

1998 Tornadoes in Florida killed at least 42 people, injured more than 260, and left hundreds homeless on 23 February.

1998 A mudslide caused by heavy rain swamped the town of Sarno, Italy, in early May, killing at least 135 people. The "black tide" of mud swept away trees and cars, blocked roads, and destroyed houses, making 2,000 people homeless.

1998 A heat wave killed at least 2,500 people in India in May and early June.

1998 The Yangtze River, China, flooded from June to August. The floods affected an estimated 230 million people and 3,656 people died.

1998 A tsunami (tidal wave) struck Papua New Guinea on 17 July, killing at least 2,500 people.

1998 Floods along the River Nile in Sudan in September and October destroyed more than 120,000 homes, leaving at least 200,000 people homeless. At least 88 people died.

1998 Hurricane Mitch devastated Central America in October, producing winds up to 240 kmh (150 mph) and causing widespread flooding and mudslides. More than 1.5 million people were made homeless, at least 8,600 people were killed, and 12,000 were unaccounted for.

1999 At least 10,000 were killed in Venezuela by floods and mudslides caused by torrential rains in December. The government proclaimed it the country's worst natural disaster of the century.

2000 Tornadoes swept through Georgia, USA, shortly after midnight on 14 February, killing 18 people and injuring about 100.

2000 In February, freak torrential rain in southern Africa caused the worst floods for 50 years in Mozambique. More than a million people were forced to leave their homes. Cyclone Eline hit the coast of Mozambique on 22 February, producing winds up to 257 kmh (160 mph) and compounding the country's problems.

WEATHER WEBSITES

http://www.discovery.com/guides/weather/weather.html
   Discovery Channel's extreme weather guide

http://www.hurricanehunters.com
   Hurricane Hunters – see photos taken from flights through the eyes of hurricanes

http://rsd.gsfc.nasa.gov/rsd/images
   Catalogue of satellite pictures of hurricanes

http://www.meto.govt.uk/sec6/sec6.html
   Links to official meteorological websites around the world

http://www.stormchaser.niu.edu/chaser/photo.html
   Storm Chaser's Photo Gallery – links to pictures taken by tornado chasers

http://weather.yahoo.com
   Weather forecasts for anywhere in the world

INDEX

ACKNOWLEDGMENTS

Dorling Kindersley would like to thank the following people for their help with this book: Caroline Greene, Amanda Rayner and Selina Wood for editorial assistance; Lester Cheeseman and Robin Hunter for design help; Mount Washington Observatory for their picture of rime frost; Bedrock Studios Ltd and Firelight Productions for computer graphics; Chris Bernstein for the index; and tornado-chaser Ian Wittmeyer for risking life and limb.

Dorling Kindersley would also like to thank the following for their kind permission to reproduce their photographs:

c=centre; l=left; r=right; b=bottom; t=top

Ardea London Ltd: Jean-Paul Ferrero 44br; **Associated Press Ap:** Agencia Estado 52bl; **Johnny Autry:** Johnny Autry 24tr; **Bridgeman Art Library, London/New York:** 7cr; **British Airways:** 6br; **Camera Press:** Hoflinger 27br; **Bruce Coleman Ltd:** 17cra; Jeff Foott 17tr; Thomas Buchholz 61tr; Tore Hagman 16–17; **Colorific!:** Alon Reininger/Contact 53bl; Michael Melford 56bc; Raghub/R Singh 5tl; Rich Frishman/Picture Group 56cl; **Corbis UK Ltd:** 46bl; Bettmann/CORBIS 37br; **Ecoscene:** 21br; Sally Morgan 21c; **Fortean Picture Library:** Werner Burger 24br; **FLPA – Images of nature:** C Carvalho 49cla; Catherine Y M Mullen 36–7; D Hoadley title page; Robin Chittenden 5crb; Tom and Pam Gardner 42cr; W Wisniewski 43 main

image; **Ian Wittmeyer:** 26cl, 26bl, 27 tr, 28cl; **Magnum:** Steve McCurry 35l, 42b; **Gene Moore:** 40bl; **Mount Washington Observatory:** 36bl; **N.A.S.A.:** 6cra, 22bl, 30cl, 30–31, 52c, 56–57, 57br; **NOAA:** George E Marshall Album 46–47; **Oxford Scientific Films:** Alastair Shay 9ca; Bob Campbell, Survival Anglia 47br; Daniel Valla 13cr; David M Dennis 51tr; Ian West 11c; Joan Root 43tl; John Brown 13tr; Martyn Chillmaid 22tr; Muzz Murray 9tc; NASA 4–5; Richard Kolar/Earth Sciences 36br; Stan Osolinski 13tl; Warren Faidley 18b, 27c, 40cb, 52–53; **Palm Beach Post:** C J Walker 32b; **Panos Pictures:** Dominic Harcourt-Webster 46br; **Planet Earth Pictures:** Adam Jones 17cr; Howard Platt 16–17; Jean Guichard 18t; Steve Bloom 24cl; **Powerstock Photolibrary/Zefa:** 42tr, 55crb; **Rex Features:** 55tl; Sipa 28bl; **Science Photo Library:** Jack

Finch 50l; David Nunuk 48–49; David Parker 49ca; David Weintraub 54–55; Earth Satellite Corporation 34cl; ESA 58–59b; Europeab Space Agency 9bl; Frank Zollo 17tl; Fred K Smith 4bl; George Post 16c, 40–41; Hank Morgan 60–61; Jerry Mason 44cl; Jerry Schad 49br; John Mead 2–3, 17crb, 60–61t; Keith Kent 23, 25; Magrath/ Folsom 16tr; Michael Giannechi 51br; N.A.S.A. 6–7, 7br, 45bl, 50cr; National Center for Atmospheric Research 41bl; NCAR 41br; Pekka Parviainen 17br, 37tr, 49bl, 51cr, 51l, 51t, 62–63; Peter Menzel 24bl; Tom van Sant 10cl; W. Bacon 38bl; **SOHO-EIT Consortium (ESA/NASA):** 4cl; **Frank Spooner Pictures:** 55cr; Carlos Angel 35cr; L. Mayer/Liaison 34tr; Noel Quidu 34b; Patrick Aventurier 56clb; **Still Pictures:** Anne Piantanida 10–11; Carl R Sang II 12tc; Denis Bringard 11br; Dennis Bringard 11cr, 11crb; Fred Bruemmer 18c; John

Kiefler 61br; Julio Etcharit 5cra; Julio Etchert 58–59; M & C Denis-Huot 19; Luiz C Marigo 11cb; **The Stock Market:** 33t; **Stock Shot:** Tony Harrington 39tr; **Tony Stone Images:** Alan R Moller 26–27; Alan R. Moller 29; Cameron Davidson 32tr; David R Frazier 44–45; E D Pritchard 12–13; Ed Pritchard 33br; Gary Holscher 37cr; Gerben Oppermans 38tr; Graeme Norways 17br; Jake Evans 39tl; Johan Elzenga 63br; John Chard 10–11; Kennan Harvey 8l; Marc Muench 20–21; Nadia Mackensie 61c; Oliver Strewe 58bl; Paul Kenward 8; Theo Allots 5br; Wayne Eastep 6bl; **Sygma:** 59br; Christian Simonpietri 45bl; J. Reed 28cr; **Telegraph Colour Library:** 38–39; **Topham Picturepoint:** Permdhai Vesmaporn 59tr; **Weatherstock/Warren Faidley:** 17cl; **Ian Wittmeyer:** 26cl, 26clb, 27tr, 28cl; **Zefa Picture Library:** 21tr.